I AM

A

MAN

MARCHING
to the MOUNTAINTOP

MARCHING
to the
MOUNTAINTOP

How Poverty, Labor Fights, and Civil Rights
Set the Stage for Martin Luther King, Jr.'s Final Hours

Ann Bausum

With a foreword by Reverend James Lawson

NATIONAL GEOGRAPHIC
WASHINGTON, DC

For the people of Memphis, and for blacks and whites everywhere who
have fought against racism, including my fourth-grade teacher—
Christine Warren—who was on the front lines of school integration in 1966-67.
All that, and you helped me love to read, too! Thank you, Mrs. Warren! —AB

The publisher and author gratefully acknowledge the review
of proofs for this book by historian Michael K. Honey. For
more information on the topic, consult Professor Honey's
definitive, award-winning account of the history, *Going
Down Jericho Road: The Memphis Strike, Martin Luther
King's Last Campaign* (W. W. Norton & Company, 2007).

Published by the National Geographic Society

John M. Fahey, Jr., CHAIRMAN OF THE BOARD
AND CHIEF EXECUTIVE OFFICER
Timothy T. Kelly, PRESIDENT
Declan Moore, EXECUTIVE VICE PRESIDENT;
PRESIDENT, PUBLISHING
Melina Gerosa Bellows, EXECUTIVE VICE PRESIDENT;
CHIEF CREATIVE OFFICER, BOOKS, KIDS, AND FAMILY

Prepared by the Book Division

Nancy Laties Feresten, SENIOR VICE PRESIDENT,
EDITOR IN CHIEF, CHILDREN'S BOOKS
Jonathan Halling, DESIGN DIRECTOR,
BOOKS AND CHILDREN'S PUBLISHING
Jay Sumner, DIRECTOR OF PHOTOGRAPHY,
CHILDREN'S PUBLISHING
Jennifer Emmett, EDITORIAL DIRECTOR,
CHILDREN'S BOOKS
Carl Mehler, DIRECTOR OF MAPS
R. Gary Colbert, PRODUCTION DIRECTOR
Jennifer A. Thornton, MANAGING EDITOR

Staff for This Book

Jennifer Emmett, PROJECT EDITOR
Eva Absher, ART DIRECTOR
Lori Epstein, SENIOR ILLUSTRATIONS EDITOR
Marty Ittner, DESIGNER
Grace Hill, ASSOCIATE MANAGING EDITOR
Joan Gossett, PRODUCTION EDITOR
Lewis R. Bassford, PRODUCTION MANAGER
Susan Borke, LEGAL AND BUSINESS AFFAIRS
Kate Olesin, EDITORIAL ASSISTANT
Kathryn Robbins, DESIGN PRODUCTION ASSISTANT
Hillary Moloney, ILLUSTRATIONS ASSISTANT

Manufacturing and Quality Management

Christopher A. Liedel, CHIEF FINANCIAL OFFICER
Phillip L. Schlosser, SENIOR VICE PRESIDENT
Chris Brown, TECHNICAL DIRECTOR
Nicole Elliott, MANAGER
Rachel Faulise, MANAGER
Robert L. Barr, MANAGER

COVER: The cover illustration combines a view taken
of Martin Luther King, Jr., on the day before his death
with a scene of striking Memphis workers before the
attempted protest of March 28, 1968. Endpapers replicate
popular protest signs from Memphis civil rights events in
1968. Pickets march past armed troops on March 29, 1968
(title page). Garbage accumulates in the street of an African-
American neighborhood in 1968 (table of contents).

The National Geographic Society is one of the
world's largest nonprofit scientific and educational
organizations. Founded in 1888 to "increase and
diffuse geographic knowledge," the Society works
to inspire people to care about the planet. National
Geographic reflects the world through its maga-
zines, television programs, films, music and radio,
books, DVDs, maps, exhibitions, live events, school
publishing programs, interactive media and merchandise. *National
Geographic* magazine, the Society's official journal, published in
English and 33 local-language editions, is read by more than 38
million people each month. The National Geographic Channel
reaches 320 million households in 34 languages in 166 countries.
National Geographic Digital Media receives more than 15 million
visitors a month. National Geographic has funded more than 9,400
scientific research, conservation and exploration projects and supports
an education program promoting geography literacy. For more
information, visit nationalgeographic.com.

For more information, please call 1-800-NGS LINE
(647-5463) or write to the following address:
National Geographic Society
1145 17th Street N.W.
Washington, D.C. 20036-4688 U.S.A.

Visit us online at www.nationalgeographic.com/books

For librarians and teachers: www.ngchildrensbooks.org
More for kids from National Geographic:
kids.nationalgeographic.com

For information about special discounts for bulk purchases,
please contact National Geographic Books Special Sales:
ngspecsales@ngs.org

For rights or permissions inquiries, please contact National
Geographic Books Subsidiary Rights: ngbookrights@ngs.org

Library of Congress Cataloging-in-Publication Data

Bausum, Ann.
Marching to the mountaintop : how poverty, labor fights, and civil
rights set the stage for Martin Luther King, Jr.'s final hours /
by Ann Bausum. — 1st ed.
   p. cm.
Includes bibliographical references and index.
ISBN 978-1-4263-0939-7 (hardcover : alk. paper) --
ISBN 978-1-4263-0940-3 (library binding : alk. paper)
1. King, Martin Luther, Jr., 1929-1968—Juvenile literature. 2. King,
Martin Luther, Jr., 1929-1968—Assassination—Juvenile literature.
3. Sanitation Workers Strike, Memphis, Tenn., 1968—Juvenile
literature. 4. Labor movement—Tennessee—Memphis—History—
20th century—Juvenile literature. 5. African Americans—Tennessee—Memphis—Social conditions—20th century—Juvenile
literature. 6. Memphis (Tenn.)—Race relations—History—20th
century—Juvenile literature. I. Title.
E185.97.K5B38 2012
323.092--dc23
[B]
                    2011024661

Text copyright © 2012 Ann Bausum.
Compilation copyright © 2012 National Geographic Society.
All rights reserved. Reproduction of the whole or any part of the contents
without written permission from the publisher is prohibited.

Printed in China
11/CCOS/1

CONTENTS

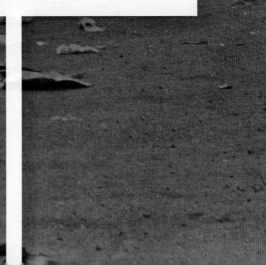

By Reverend James Lawson

There are very rare, peculiar moments in history when we humans are allowed to catch a glimpse at the vision of a fairer world, and when we experience the nobility and joy of being fully alive as children of life. This book, *Marching to the Mountaintop,* describes such a moment in the emergence of a nonviolent direct action movement (the intensified years in the journey of Martin Luther King, Jr., 1953-1973, and the garbage workers' strike of Memphis 1968).

Ann Bausum has given us a beautiful and inspiring account capturing much of the drama of our struggle in a comprehensive fashion and also pointing us toward the larger frame of what is called the civil rights movement. I hope that you will drink deeply from the portrait of Dr. King—my Moses and colleague from 1955 to 1968. I urge you to also hear and feel the character, courage, and compassion of the 1,300 workers who had the temerity to insist "I am a man."

I like to call the civil rights movement the second American revolution. The first one in 1776 excluded the human rights of women, Native Americans, millions of slaves, black people, Mexican Americans, Chinese Americans, and others. The second one was largely nonviolent (a concept coined by Mohandas K. Gandhi, the father of the science of nonviolent social change) and effectively caused our Constitution to be declared as including all residents of our land.

All through this book, you will see the sheer human dignity of ordinary people, younger and older, provoked by the example of the 1,300 workers and their wives and families. These working families did not allow the nature of their daily hard labor and its ethos of racism to blot out their humanity or their insistence that one day their work would lift them out of abject poverty. This quest for human dignity—equality, liberty, and justice for all—is the soul of the sanitation strike and the civil rights movement. After all, we humans have been birthed to be human—in the likeness of God. Nothing less can even begin to satisfy our lives.

The Memphis strike was not the last mass direct action campaign of that era. It was the last campaign in which Dr. King participated. In 1969 we

Martin Luther King, Jr., and James Lawson became allies in the fight for African-American rights from their first meeting in 1957. At King's urging, Lawson used his keen understanding of the power of nonviolence to train many of the young people who went on to play significant roles in the civil rights movement. In 1968, Lawson (above, holding sign) collaborated with King, local youths, labor leaders, and other supporters to champion the need for workers to receive fair treatment from "King Henry," Memphis mayor Henry Loeb.

Memphians were again engaged in a massive direct action effort, which began the restructuring of our public schools. More than 200,000 people, including more than 70,000 students, participated. Because of that campaign, I, and others, spent Christmas 1969 in the county jail.

I hope that you the readers will see yourselves in these pages. Our work for human dignity and truth is not over. Each generation must do its share. Racism, sexism, violence, greed, and materialism are still with us. You must continue the personal and community nonviolent march toward the promised land.

A Note From the Publisher: Reverend Lawson's views on the assassination of Martin Luther King, Jr., differ from the account offered in this book, which is based on the official record of the investigation. Drawing on other information, some historians, including Reverend Lawson, believe there are errors in this record. History is not fixed, and controversy is useful. We challenge all budding historians to seek to uncover the truth of this investigation and other historical episodes that further our understanding of ourselves. To read the trial records and draw your own conclusions, please consult The 13th Juror *(CreateSpace, 2009).*

**"Nobody knows the trouble I've seen,
Nobody knows my sorrow.
Nobody knows the trouble I've seen.
Glory, hallelujah!"**

Chorus from a freedom song based
on an African-American spiritual

As I remember it, the chore of taking out the trash fell to me every week of my childhood. My family might disagree, but if anything could trick my memory into believing this statistic it is my recollection of the garbage itself. Pungent. Disgusting. Foul. Unforgettable.

Back then, garbage was truly garbage. To take out the trash during the 1960s meant to get up close and personal with a week's worth of refuse in the most intimate and repulsive of ways. No one had yet invented plastic garbage-can liners or the wheeled trash cans we have today. At that time our family's garbage went into aluminum cans with clanging metal lids. And the garbage went in naked.

In 1968, when I was ten years old, people really cooked. Recipes started with raw ingredients, and the garbage can told the tales of the week's menu. Onion skins, carrot peelings, and apple cores. The grease from the morning's bacon. Half-eaten food scraped from plates in the evening. The wet, smelly, slippery bones of the chicken carcass that had been boiled for soup stock. Mold-fuzzy bread. Spoiled fruit. Slimy potato peels. Scum-coated eggshells. Then add yesterday's newspapers. Used Kleenex. Cat-food cans lined with sticky juices. Everything went into the same metal can out the back door of our home in Virginia.

The story of our garbage multiplied itself to infinity at homes throughout the nation. In communities where temperatures soared, garbage baked in the summer heat like some witch's stew until foul odors broadcast its location, flies bred on the vapors, and maggots hatched in the waste. Wet, raw, saturated with rancid smells that lingered long after the diesel-powered truck had lumbered away: That was the garbage of the 1960s. The people who collected the trash were always male, and we called them, simply, garbagemen.

It's universal: Young people take out the trash everywhere, including in Memphis during the 1968 strike.

This book is about the story of garbage in one city—Memphis, Tennessee—and the lives of the men tasked with collecting it during 1968. These men, all of whom were African American, labored brutally hard for such meager wages that many of them qualified for welfare. Six days a week they followed their noses to garbage cans (curbside trash collection had yet to become the norm); then they manhandled the waste to the street using giant washtubs. The city-supplied tubs corroded with time, leaving their bottoms so peppered with holes that garbage slop dripped onto the bodies and clothes of the city's garbagemen as they labored.

During the 1960s the sanitation workers of Memphis showed up for work every day knowing they would be treated like garbage. By the end of the day they smelled and felt like garbage, too. Unfairness guided their employment, and racism ruled their workdays. So passed the lives of the garbagemen of Memphis until something snapped, one day in February 1968, and the men collectively declared, "Enough is enough." Accumulated injustices, compounded by an unexpected tragedy, fueled their determination. Just like that they went out on strike, setting in motion a series of events that would transform their lives, upend the city of Memphis, and lead to the death of the nation's most notable—and perhaps most hated—advocate for civil rights.

Labor relations, human dignity, and a test of stubborn wills drove developments that spring in Memphis, Tennessee. Behind this union of worker rights and civil rights stood the men expected to handle one ever present substance: garbage.

CAST OF CHARACTERS

Southern Christian Leadership Conference

In 1957, heartened by the successful outcome of the Montgomery bus boycott, key organizers team up with colleagues from other communities to form the Southern Christian Leadership Conference, or SCLC, and advocate for social change through the use of nonviolence. Key participants:

Martin Luther King, Jr., president from 1957 until his death in 1968.

Ralph D. Abernathy, treasurer, King's closest colleague, and the man who succeeds him as organization president.

Lieutenants, such as **Hosea Williams** and **Jesse Jackson** (standing left and center with **King** and **Abernathy** at the Lorraine Motel in Memphis, April 3, 1968), as well as **Bernard Lee, James Orange,** and **Andrew Young.**

Authorities

Lyndon B. Johnson, President of the United States (1963-1969).

J. Edgar Hoover, director of the Federal Bureau of Investigation (FBI) and the chief force behind FBI campaigns to spy on and discredit Martin Luther King, Jr.

Former FBI agent **Frank Holloman,** director of the Memphis fire and police departments, and the department's 800 officers, including undercover staffers **Marrell "Max" McCullough, Ed Redditt,** and **Willie Richmond.**

The Memphis Movement

On February 24, 1968, local clergy establish a strike-support organization called Community on the Move for Equality, or COME.

James Lawson, an associate of King's with deep experience in the use of nonviolence and a local Methodist minister, becomes the group's leader.

Other key organizing ministers include Presbyterian **Ezekiel Bell,** Clayborn Temple's white leader **Malcom Blackburn,** Baptist minister and local judge **Benjamin Hooks,** AME leader **H. Ralph Jackson,** Baptist minister **James Jordan,** Baptist minister **Samuel "Billy" Kyles,** Baptist minister and youth organizer **Harold Middlebrook,** and AME minister **Henry Starks** (president of the association of local African-American ministers).

Charles Cabbage (left) and **Coby Smith** (right), who had founded the Black Organizing Project (BOP) in 1967, question the exclusive use of nonviolence as a force for change; they maintain an uneasy alliance with COME, especially after setting up a militant offshoot to BOP known as the Invaders with associates such as **Calvin Taylor.**

Other notable strike supporters include local activist **Cornelia Crenshaw, Dick Moon** (the university chaplain who mounts a hunger strike in April 1968), **Maxine Smith** (executive director of the local chapter of the NAACP), NAACP president **Jesse Turner,** and white Methodist minister **Frank McRae** (who tries to persuade the Memphis mayor to settle the strike).

Labor

Public workers organize the American Federation of State, County and Municipal Employees, or AFSCME, during the 1930s. By 1968 the organization represents almost 400,000 members in nearly 2,000 local chapters, including Memphis Local 1733.

 T. O. Jones, president of AFSCME Local 1733, who helped found the fledgling union in 1963, stands in the front lines throughout the 1968 strike.

 Jerry Wurf, international president of the union since 1964, assumes personal responsibility as the advocate for members of Local 1733.

 AFSCME field services director **P. J. Ciampa** serves as the union's chief liaison with the striking workers.

 Other key national players from AFSCME include union organizer **Jesse Epps** (left), **Bill Lucy** (the highest ranking African American at AFSCME in 1968), and **Joe Paisley** (the Tennessee representative for AFSCME).

Workers such as **Robert Beasley, Clinton Burrows, Ed Gillis, J. L. McClain, James Robinson, Taylor Rogers, Joe Warren,** and **Haley Williams** are among the **1,300 men** who fight for recognition as human beings and as members of a union; the vast majority are sanitation workers (1,100), but another 230 hold jobs in the sewer and drainage division of the department of public works.

Other local labor supporters include members of the United Rubber Workers Union (Local 186), **Taylor Blair** (a white union agent who advocates settlement), **Tommy Powell** (president of the Memphis Labor Council and a local white), and **Bill Ross** (a white who leads the local council of AFL-CIO affiliates).

Management

 Henry Loeb, mayor of Memphis, 1968-1972, former local business owner, former public works commissioner (1956-1960), and former mayor (1960-1963).

Memphis City Council, thirteen members elected for service beginning January 1968 to fill seven district seats and six at-large seats, including twelve men (three of whom are African American) and one woman.

Charles Blackburn, director of the Memphis department of public works, which employs sanitation and street workers.

Mediators

James Reynolds, U.S. Department of Labor undersecretary (wearing glasses, back to camera, seated with, counterclockwise, AFSCME representatives **Bill Lucy, Jerry Wurf,** and **P. J. Ciampa**).

Frank Miles (far left), Memphis labor advocate and local businessperson.

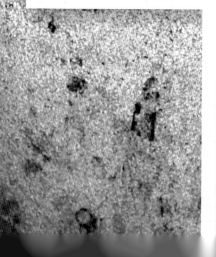

Chapter 1

DEATH
IN MEMPHIS

"It was horrible," said the woman.

One minute she could see a sanitation worker struggling to climb out of the refuse barrel of a city garbage truck. The next minute mechanical forces pulled him back into the cavernous opening. It looked to her as though the man's raincoat had snagged on the vehicle, foiling his escape attempt. "His body went in first and his legs were hanging out," said the eyewitness, who had been sitting at her kitchen table in Memphis, Tennessee, when the truck paused in front of her home. Next, she watched the man's legs vanish as the motion of the truck's compacting unit swept the worker toward his death. "The big thing just swallowed him," she reported.

We shall overcome. We shall overcome. We shall overcome some day-ay-ay-ay-ay. Deep in my heart, I do believe, We shall overcome some day.

Freedom song adapted from a gospel hymn
for a southern labor fight during the 1940s

In 1968 many Memphis residents stored their trash in uncovered 50-gallon drums. Frequent rains added to the soupy, unsavory nature of the garbage that workers transferred to waiting trucks. The exclusively African-American workforce took its orders from white supervisors (below).

Unbeknownst to Mrs. C. E. Hinson, another man was already trapped inside the vibrating truck body. Before vehicle driver Willie Crain could react, Echol Cole, age 36, and Robert Walker, age 30, would be crushed to death. Nobody ever identified which one came close to escaping.

Cole and Walker wore raincoats for good reason on February 1, 1968. At the end of a wet workday, Willie Crain's four-man crew had divvied up the truck's available shelter for the trip to the garbage dump. Elester Gregory and Eddie Ross, Jr., squeezed into the driver's cab with Crain and left the younger members of the crew with two choices. They could hold on tight to exterior perches while the truck passed through torrential rains. Or they could climb inside the truck's garbage barrel, wedged between the front wall of the vessel and the packing arm that pressed a load of refuse against the rear of the truck. Walker and Cole opted for the dryer and seemingly more secure interior space.

Rain or shine, the 1,100 sanitation workers of Memphis collected what amounted to 2,500 tons of garbage a day. This all-male, exclusively African-American staff worked six days a week with one 15-minute break for lunch and no routine access to bathroom facilities. Their pay was based on their garbage routes, not their hours worked, so there was no overtime compensation when the days ran long. Workers supplied their own clothing and gloves, toted rain-saturated garbage in leaky tubs supplied by the city, and had no place to shower or to change out of soiled clothes before returning home. Even though the men worked full-time, their earnings failed to lift their families from poverty. To make ends meet, many found extra jobs, paid for groceries with government-sponsored food stamps, lived in low-income housing projects, and made use of items scavenged during their garbage runs.

The men toiled under a system with eerie echoes of the pre–Civil War South, what some called the plantation mentality. Whites worked as supervisors. Blacks, who made up almost 40 percent of the city's population, performed the

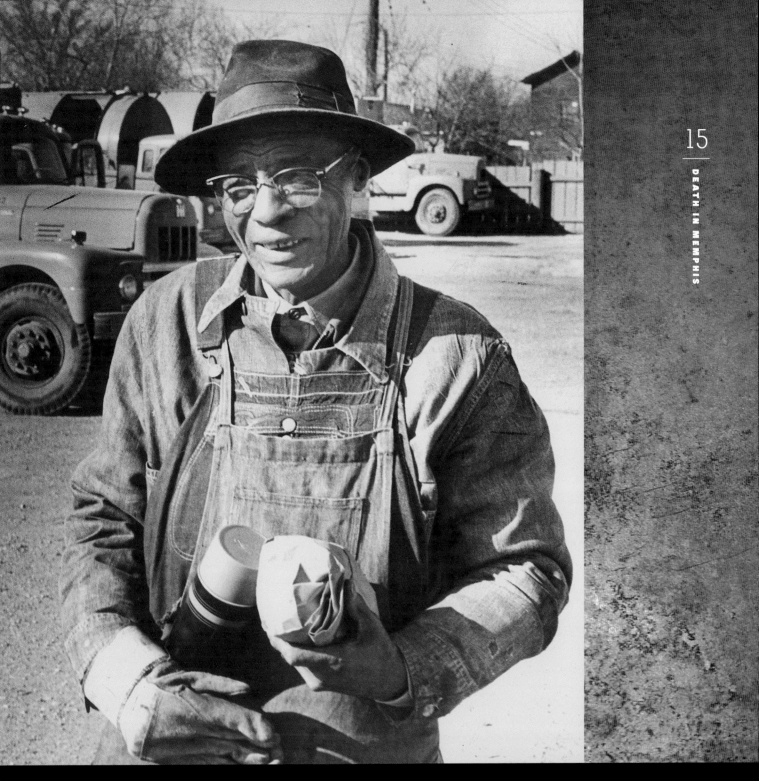

Memphis residents, or Memphians, called their sanitation workers garbagemen, walking buzzards, and tub toters, a name that reflected the washtubs they used for ferrying garbage from backyard storage barrels to city trucks. Workers (above, R. J. Sanders) balanced the large tubs on their heads or pushed them in three-wheeled carts.

backbreaking labor. Bosses expected to be addressed as "sir." Workers endured being called "boy," regardless of their ages. Whites presumed to know what was best for "our Negroes," and blacks tolerated poor treatment for fear of losing their jobs, or worse. City officials had no motivation to recognize the fledgling labor union that sought to protect the workers and to advocate for their rights. As a result, employees "acted like they were working on a plantation, doing what the master said," recalled sanitation worker Clinton Burrows.

Garbage collectors faced back injuries and other strains because of the physical demands of the work, and they fretted about the use of unsafe equipment. Willie Crain's truck had been purchased on the cheap in 1957 at a time when Henry Loeb ran the department of public works. By 1968, when Loeb returned to public office as the newly elected Memphis mayor, the city had begun replacing the old trucks. Two of the vehicles, including Crain's truck, had been retrofitted with a makeshift motor after the unit's trash-compacting engine had worn out. As best as anyone could figure after the deaths of Echol Cole and Robert Walker, a loose shovel had fallen into the wiring for the replacement motor and had accidentally triggered the reversal of the trash compactor.

Like those of other sanitation workers, the families of Cole and Walker managed paycheck to paycheck, leaving no reserves for emergencies. Their jobs came without the benefits of life insurance or a guarantee of support in the case of work-related injury or death. Mayor Loeb honored the victims by lowering public flags to half-mast, but he offered scant assistance to their survivors. The city contributed $500 toward the men's $900 funerals and paid out an extra month's wages to Cole's widow and the widow of Walker (who was pregnant).

The deaths of Cole and Walker wrapped up a particularly bad week for African Americans employed at the department of public works. This unit handled garbage collection, street repairs, and other city maintenance. On January 30, two days before the sanitation-worker fatalities, 21 members of the sewer and drainage division had been sent home with only two hours of "show-up pay" because of bad weather. The previous public works director had kept staff employed regardless of the weather, but Mayor Loeb had ordered Charles Blackburn, his new director, to return to Loeb's old rainy-day policy from the 1950s. In a climate where rain fell frequently, workers lost their ability to predict their income. "That's when we commenced starving," explained road worker Ed Gillis.

Street workers turned to Thomas Oliver Jones for help. T. O. Jones was among 33 sanitation workers who had started a strike in 1963 and lost their jobs. When officials were pressured to rehire the workers, Jones refused to rejoin the force. Over time he established a fledgling union for public works employees and gained recognition for his small group by the American Federation of State, County and Municipal Employees, better known as AFSCME. Jones's group called itself Local 1733 in honor of the 33 men fired during the 1963 strike. Jones tried to lead another walkout in 1966. This time 500 workers agreed to strike, but the work stoppage collapsed after a local judge declared the strike

THERE wasn't too much opportunity for a black man at that time. Really wasn't no other jobs hardly to be found. I was at a point I had to take what I could get.

Taylor Rogers, who became a Memphis sanitation worker about 1959

illegal. "All city employees may not strike for any purpose whatsoever," the judge declared. This injunction, or prohibition against striking, had never been challenged in court, so it remained in force and discouraged further strikes. Nonetheless, Jones continued to quietly recruit members for Local 1733 and became its unofficial spokesperson.

Jones raised the men's rainy-day concerns with Charles Blackburn and left the meeting thinking the public works director had agreed to pay the 21 men their missing wages. Blackburn said he would reconsider the rainy-day policy, too, and, within a few days, he instructed supervisors to try to keep everyone fully employed regardless of the weather. During that same period, Panfilo Julius Ciampa, field director for Washington, D.C.-based AFSCME, visited Memphis. Jones arranged for his union contact to meet the new public works

The men toiled under a system with eerie echoes of the pre–Civil War South, what some called the plantation mentality. Whites worked as supervisors. Blacks performed the backbreaking labor.

By 1968 the city of Memphis had replaced most of its garbage trucks with a rear-loading model (above, carrying unidentified workers). Echol Cole and Robert Walker died in an older side-loading vehicle nicknamed the wiener barrel because of its rounded shape. Their fatalities followed the deaths of two other sanitation workers during a 1964 truck rollover accident.

director on February 1. P. J. Ciampa learned that Blackburn was a personal friend of the newly elected mayor and had gained appointment to the job after an unrelated career in insurance work. He would later describe Blackburn as "a guy who didn't know a sanitation truck from a wheelbarrow."

Their afternoon meeting took place shortly before

Willie Crain's truck began crushing two sanitation workers to death. Jones learned of the accident almost immediately. As he drove back from taking Ciampa to the Memphis airport, Jones followed a hunch that trouble was brewing and pursued an emergency public works vehicle that turned out to be racing toward the reported accident. Events snowballed as the news spread. Surviving workers knew they could just as easily have lost their own lives. They grew offended when the city didn't cover the full costs of burying the victims. They fretted over the potential for lost wages during bad weather. They worried about how to survive on the money they earned even at full employment. And they fumed when the 21 workers opened their pay envelopes the following week and discovered no boost in pay for the rainy day of January 30.

Something snapped—or perhaps ignited—under the weight of these pressures in a system run with that plantation-style mind-set. In theory, slavery had ended 100 years earlier, but blacks in Memphis during 1968 had more in common with African-American slaves who had worked the region's cotton fields than with the whites who ran Memphis businesses, served in city government, and covered the local news. Even poor whites, thanks to decades of segregated southern living, focused more attention on their racial superiority over blacks than the common interests they and blacks could have pursued through unions for higher wages and better working conditions. Poverty, racial isolation, and a history of voter intimidation left blacks underrepresented and their needs ignored.

"Nobody listens" to black people, observed Maxine Smith, executive director of the Memphis branch of the NAACP. "Nobody listened to us and the garbage men through the years. For some reason, our city government demands a crisis" before noticing African-American concerns.

Whites may not have seen it coming, but a crisis of epic proportions loomed on the horizon for Memphis, Tennessee.

Chapter 2

STRIKE!

"I'm ready to go to jail," announced union organizer T. O. Jones. "Why are you going to jail?" asked Charles Blackburn. Jones, having excused himself to change into khaki pants—jail clothes—reminded the new public works director of the court injunction that prohibited strikes by Memphis public workers. Blackburn had offered no resolution of the list of demands Jones had just shared with him, demands that he had developed earlier that evening during a meeting with more than 700 department workers. Key principles included union recognition, pay increases, overtime compensation, full employment regardless of weather, and improved worker safety. Now Jones knew the men would strike.

Oh, workers can you stand it? Oh, tell me how you can.
Will you be a lousy scab, or will you be a man?
Which side are you on, oh, which side are you on?
Which side are you on, oh, which side are you on?

Verse from a labor song written in 1932
by Florence Patton Reece, a coal miner's wife

Among the ways mayor Henry Loeb (left, walking with striking workers to their February 13 meeting) offended blacks was to mispronounce *Negro*, the era's term for African Americans, as the racism-laced *Nigra*. In 1968 blacks refused to contribute their garbage for collection by strike-breaking workers. Uncollected, the waste accumulated by the week (above).

" **H** e gives us nothing, we'll give him nothing,"** yelled one of the men when waiting workers learned of Blackburn's stance. Those gathered held no official vote on whether or not to strike; they just reached a collective agreement to quit working. Maybe city officials would take notice if the garbage stopped being picked up and road repairs ceased.

The next morning, empty work barns must have erased whatever illusions Blackburn held about the submissiveness of his workforce. Only 170 of the city's 1,100 garbage workers reported for duty on Monday, February 12. Just 16 members of the 230-man street crew appeared. Almost without warning, more than 85 percent of the workforce had failed to show up for work. The numbers were even worse the next day. Some workers had reported on Monday because they hadn't heard about the strike. Now they joined the walkout, too. Peer pressure kept others off the job. If employees kept working, they knew they'd hear about it back in the neighborhoods and churches they shared with the strikers. Better to stay home. Hundreds of enthusiastic men rushed to join the union.

Public Works Director Blackburn struggled to organize his skeletal workforce into the five-man crews required to run a garbage truck. On Monday he managed to staff 38 garbage trucks, leaving as many as 150 vehicles idle for the day. By Wednesday he could fill only four. Every truck required a police escort in order to ensure that striking workers wouldn't harass those few men who had stayed on the job.

P. J. Ciampa groaned at his AFSCME office on Monday when he learned of the Memphis walkout. This veteran organizer of countless labor strikes knew the Memphis timing was all wrong. Garbage strikes worked best in hot weather when garbage smelled its worst. Plus, city leaders would find it easy in February to hire unemployed agricultural workers to break the strike. And how were workers going to feed their families when their paychecks stopped coming? Usually union dues supported a strike fund, but Local 1733's small membership

Holes peppered the corroded bottoms of many city-supplied washtubs, so garbage slop dripped onto the bodies and clothes of sanitation workers as they toiled. Tubs rested unused (above) during the 1968 strike. The Memphis action began just as a nine-day garbage strike ended in New York City (right, sweeping up some accumulated trash).

base had created few assets. Furthermore, because southern business leaders and politicians disliked unions, the South was the hardest place to win a strike. On top of it all, in the face of an unexpected strike, public support would probably favor the newly elected leaders of Memphis. Never strike in anger, AFSCME officials always advised, and strike only when victory is certain. The Memphis strike looked like a disaster.

Tell the men to go back to work, Ciampa told Memphis labor leader Bill Ross by telephone. Ross refused, explaining that he had never seen such a determined group of men. "I said, buddy, I'm the only one white man in this building with 1,300 black souls out there. I'm not about to go out there and tell those people to go back to work. Now if you want to tell them to go back to work, you come down here and you do it yourself."

Almost immediately the AFSCME field director flew to Memphis. By Monday night, three other AFSCME staffers had arrived, including Bill Lucy, a black Memphis native pulled from an assignment in Michigan. After meeting on Tuesday with Mayor Henry Loeb and with a room full of striking workers, Ciampa realized that nobody, not even T. O. Jones, could have stopped the strike. Jones "had to run to stay out front," Ciampa would later say.

Ciampa could find no common ground with the mayor. Loeb insisted that negotiations take place in front of news reporters, a tough environment for reaching the compromises necessary for strike settlements. Ciampa sized up Loeb as insincere, close-minded, and happy to make comments that played well to his white citizen base while avoiding serious negotiation. Meanwhile, Ciampa, a tough-talking negotiator with an Italian-American accent, struck Loeb as rude and intrusive, and Ciampa's assertive northeastern style grated against other whites, too. After Ciampa directed a few choice comments at the mayor—"Oh, put your halo in your pocket and let's get realistic"; "Because you are mayor of Memphis it doesn't make you God"; and "Keep your big mouth shut!"—orange bumper stickers reading "Ciampa Go Home" appeared all over Memphis. Within days AFSCME international director Jerry Wurf would decide to take personal charge of the negotiations, leaving Ciampa to coordinate strategy regarding the workers.

Traditionally, striking workers would set up picket lines and march with protest signs at their places of work. Replacement laborers, known as scab workers, would have to "cross the picket lines" and face verbal harassment by strikers in order to get to work. But Ciampa's team and local union leaders worried that this aggressive approach might backfire in the racially charged South. They didn't want to give members of the city's almost entirely white police force an excuse to attack black strikers. Instead, strike organizers turned to tried-and-true forms of nonviolent civil disobedience: mass meetings, peaceful marches, boycotts, and so on. Such strategies had worked in past labor fights and were central to the ongoing civil rights movement led by Martin Luther King, Jr.

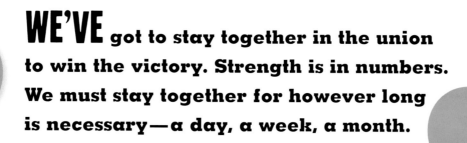

WE'VE got to stay together in the union to win the victory. Strength is in numbers. We must stay together for however long is necessary—a day, a week, a month.

P. J. Ciampa, AFSCME field director, addressing workers on February 13, 1968

The first mass march occurred the afternoon of Tuesday, February 13, day two of the strike. T. O. Jones and Bill Lucy led a formation of more than 800 workers, walking in rows of four or five men, from their union meeting place in north Memphis to downtown. They clapped, cheered, and sang freedom songs as they marched a distance of about five miles to city hall. "The men are here," Lucy told the mayor. "You said, 'Any men you want to bring down to talk to me, I'll talk to them.' Here they are." At first Loeb misunderstood the size of Lucy's group and asked him to escort the men into the mayor's office. Soon he corrected himself and met workers in a large assembly hall.

Loeb's so-called plantation-mentality approach backfired when he spoke to the workers as if they were children—humoring, scolding, and pressuring them to return to work. To the mayor's shock, the men laughed at him.

Strike organizers credited Henry Loeb (above, at desk, during early negotiations) with becoming their best ally because his attitudes and behavior united blacks (right, marching on February 23) in their opposition to the city.

26

They clapped, cheered, and sang freedom songs as they marched a distance of about five miles to city hall. "The men are here," Lucy told the mayor. "You said, 'Any men you want to bring down to talk to me, I'll talk to them.' Here they are."

When Loeb expressed his empathy for them by using the expression, "I'd give you the shirt off my back," one of the men called in reply, "Just give me a decent salary, and I'll buy my own." The workers' cheekiness and disrespect infuriated the mayor. Loeb vowed to get the garbage collected with or without the men's help. "Bet on it!" he declared as he stormed out of the meeting.

Loeb was a well-educated business-owner-turned-politician. Three generations of his family had exploited black workers and amassed a fortune in the family laundry business. His father had prevented black washerwomen from organizing a union or striking for better pay by filling their jobs from the ranks of the unemployed. Employees put up with miserable wages because some job was better than no job. When Henry Loeb became public works director in the

THIS IS just a warning. Please don't bring another damn truck out of that gate. Do you love your family? Please, please.

Anonymous note sent by a strike supporter to a worker who continued to collect garbage

1950s, he brought along his family business mind-set. As director he bought the cheapest of equipment, instituted the program of staff cuts on rainy days, justified unpaid overtime by offering paid vacation, and beat back every attempt to form unions. For Henry Loeb, the 1968 strike became a battle of wills—mayor against rebellious blacks. If he just held out long enough, he believed, the workers would give up. Early in the strike, Loeb told a white acquaintance and union advocate that his father "would turn over in his grave if he knew he had ever recognized a damn union," Taylor Blair recalled. "I knew there wasn't much point in arguing with a fellow like that because he was trying to uphold what his daddy had said."

Loeb suspended settlement negotiations soon after his first meeting with the workers, and he announced that the city would begin replacing workers two days later. To poll the striking workers, union officials asked them to stand if they wanted to keep fighting. "They stood in unison—1,000 plus. They're not going back," an AFSCME official reported. By Friday Loeb had recruited replacements for only a fraction of the missing workers. Most whites dismissed garbage collection as beneath them, and only the most desperate of African Americans agreed to work against the cause of fellow blacks.

The city developed emergency rules to cope with

the labor shortage. Trash collection dropped from twice to once a week. City officials instructed citizens to haul their trash to the curb. They encouraged families to include food waste in their trash—left uncollected it would encourage breeding of the city's persistent population of rats—but to store other trash until the strike ended. Burning garbage remained illegal. Boy Scout groups volunteered to carry garbage barrels to curbs for the elderly, or even to haul trash to emergency dump sites. Others earned cash from such chores.

Members of the city council struggled to find their roles in the growing crisis. Like the mayor, they were new to their jobs and to a weeks-old governance system. The mayor insisted that he alone could negotiate on behalf of the city, and he became angry whenever council members tried to settle the strike. The ten whites on the council (including the council's sole female member) saw little reason to challenge his authority, and the three blacks on the council lacked the political power to argue otherwise.

After the strike carried on into a second week, though, black councillor Fred Davis, chair of the city's public works committee, offered to meet with workers to discuss their grievances. The February 22 session deteriorated after union reps recruited hundreds of workers to march on city hall and crowd the council chamber. Volunteers arrived with more than 100 loaves of bread, and wives of striking workers made bologna sandwiches for the group. Workers applauded as union reps and supportive ministers spoke forcefully on their behalf, and they refused to leave without having their demands met. Committee members struggled to construct a settlement resolution that could be presented to the full council for approval the next day. It took more than an hour to persuade T. O. Jones and the men to accept the one-day delay.

Workers stood and cheered before leaving the hall. They vowed to return on February 23 for the council vote. If all went as promised, the strike would be over the next day.

Chapter 3

IMPASSE

"Let's keep marching," urged James Lawson. "They're trying to provoke us. Keep going," he said. The Methodist minister watched as a string of police cars edged closer to retreating workers. Bumper touching bumper, the cars crowded against the rows of marchers, herding them into a tighter formation. Lawson recognized the potential for conflict from his years of experience with the civil rights movement. Workers and accompanying family members needed to walk off some of their anger and disappointment over the latest city council meetings. Strikers had left city hall on February 22 anticipating a settlement of their grievances.

Are your clothes all patched and tattered?
Are you living in a shack?
Would you have your troubles scattered?
Then dump the bosses off your back.

Verse from "Dump the Bosses Off Your Back,"
a popular labor song from the early 20th century

Local AFSCME organizer T. O. Jones (above, wearing raincoat, with striking workers) promoted unions all his life. "Tell the guys to stay with the union," he advised in 1989. "The union, that's the best salvation." The support team for striking workers included AFSCME president Jerry Wurf (left, wearing glasses, as he advocates for the right to stage a protest march on February 23).

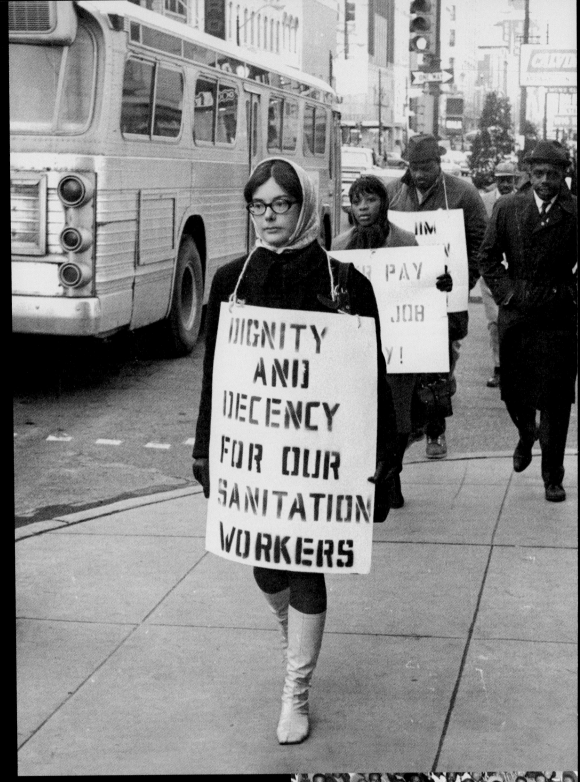

On Friday, February 23, James Lawson
(right, pointing) spoke forcefully after
city council members refused to address
the demands of striking workers. Three
days later, more than 130 workers and
supporters, including local whites (above),
took their demands to the street in silent
protest. Picket marches continued two or
three times daily for the rest of the strike.

**nstead of hearing good news on Friday, February 23,** however, workers had suffered an insulting rebuke. The full council had not even voted on the committee settlement resolution from the previous day, as had been promised. Instead, after a lengthy private meeting, council members affirmed their support of Mayor Henry Loeb's settlement terms and granted him full negotiating authority. Then they shut down the microphones, turned off the lights, and left the 1,000 or so stunned spectators to sit alone in a semidark hall. Only 4 of the 13 council members had opposed the resolution—the three African Americans and an antiunion white named Tom Todd, who favored even tougher language.

Worker fury and frustration at the vote began to lift as they started a three-mile walk to Mason Temple, but new anxieties developed as a formation of squad cars closed in on marchers. Five policemen crowded each car, clutching rifles and wooden billy clubs as they eyed the crowd. Virtually all of the city's police officers were white males who likely regarded the Memphis African Americans through the era's racist lens. At any time and without cause blacks could expect insults, harassment, and beatings during encounters with white policemen. Recent events left local police officers spoiling for the chance to pay blacks back for their defiant behavior, especially during the previous day's boisterous occupation of city hall.

"Oh! He runned over my foot!" cried Gladys Carpenter, some seven blocks into the march. One of the encroaching police cars had rolled onto her shoe, trapping it but without lasting injury. This veteran of other civil rights marches had purposely placed herself at the end of a row, thinking drivers would be less likely to crowd a female participant. Apparently not. Her companions surrounded the car, rocking it in an attempt to free her. This assertive reaction triggered an instant order: Disperse the crowd. Officers leaped from their squad cars with shouts of "Mace. Mace." Each man carried a small spray can filled with a disabling gel that combined tear gas with a chemical strong enough to peel off skin. The mixture, when sprayed on someone's face, left victims disoriented, nauseated, unable to see, and in agonizing pain.

Officers systematically attacked the strike leaders. T. O. Jones found himself accosted at gunpoint before a swarm of protective workers shielded him from harm. P. J. Ciampa heard an officer say, "Yeah, we'll take care of you." Then lawmen doused him in Mace. Ciampa fell to the ground; soon the skin beneath his left eye would start to peel away. AFSCME director Jerry Wurf, who had trouble walking because of polio, escaped attack only because he'd caught a ride. Workers rescued Ciampa and sent him and other disabled victims by car to Mason Temple.

Lawson, in keeping with his commitment to nonviolent resistance, stood his ground and received repeated blasts of the disabling spray. African-American news reporters, well-dressed ministers, striking workers, and even shoppers emerging from stores all got sprayed. "At that moment the enemy was anybody

IF THE ministers hadn't gotten into it, there would have been a lot of bloodshed . . . They was just like Martin King. They didn't want no violence.

Ed Gillis, age 72, striking worker from the Memphis sewer and drainage division of the department of public works

with a black face," noted an African-American government official who received multiple doses of Mace despite having displayed his ID badge.

"Move. Move. Move," officers yelled, even as they herded people against sidewalk storefronts so that it was harder to flee the spray. Women screamed. Marchers sought to protect their eyes with their hands or hats only to feel the liquid squirted up their noses. Cautionary calls of "Don't rub your eyes" passed through the crowd. A police supply truck arrived with gas masks for officers and four-foot-long wooden clubs. The Mace assaults gave way to random clubbing of anyone within arms' reach. Many marchers ran from the mayhem.

Lawson stayed on the scene, organized some 70 survivors of the attack into rough formation, and completed the march. Other participants straggled home or took alternative paths to the meeting point, where they rallied with passionate speeches about police brutality. In contrast, the police claimed that "a large and unruly crowd" had attacked the officers. "We think Memphians will applaud their police for the self-control they showed," noted the *Commercial Appeal.*

Before the Friday police attack "the garbage strike hadn't really caught on," recalled local NAACP director Maxine Smith. Any lack of interest vanished in the day's haze of Mace and brutality. That night, community activist Cornelia Crenshaw helped send telegrams to the city's more than 200 African-American ministers. The next morning, some 150 of them formed a strategy committee that would later become known as the strike support group called Community on the Move for Equality (COME). James Lawson was its leader. That same Saturday a local judge warned union leaders that they would be arrested if they took part in further protests, so COME activists stepped out front while union officials worked behind the scenes. "This is no longer 1,300 men fighting, but it's this whole Negro community fighting" became the mind-set, according to one union rep.

Strike organizers established an ambitious plan

to build morale, provide purpose to idle workers, and maintain pressure on the city for a settlement. Organizers promoted a boycott of white-owned downtown stores, Loeb family businesses, and the biased white newspapers. They rallied local teens to support their cause. Workers met daily at union rallies. They took turns manning a picket line that marched through downtown Memphis. Workers, family members, and supporters gathered nightly for spirited mass meetings that rotated from church to church throughout the African-American community. At these meetings and during Sunday church services, organizers collected cash and other donations for striking families, recruited volunteers, and reminded everyone to "keep your money in your pocket" for the boycott and "buy no new clothes for Easter!"

Securing funds to sustain the strike became a central task of the Memphis movement. Some 1,300 workers had lost their income by going on strike; it took thousands of dollars to keep these families fed, doctored, housed, and supplied with electricity. Donations arrived from national union offices, from local unions, and via spare change tossed into garbage cans at mass meetings.

"Mace. Mace." Each man carried a small spray can filled with a disabling gel that combined tear gas with a chemical strong enough to peel off skin. The mixture . . . left victims disoriented, nauseated, unable to see, and in agonizing pain.

Prior to 1968 the use of Mace had been restricted to military warfare. Its employment in Memphis during the public works' strike represented one of the first times law enforcement officers directed the disabling chemical at U.S. citizens.

Marchers endured multiple blasts of Mace (note man portrayed left and far left) and the use of dramatic physical force when the police confronted the assembly on February 23. Officers sprayed so much Mace at the scene that some policemen began to experience symptoms from the cloud of spray that hung in the air and wafted off of victims.

Meanwhile, the city racked up even greater strike-related expenses through police overtime and purchases of Mace and riot gear.

By late February, three weeks into the strike,

negotiations had reached an impasse. About 40 of the city's 180 garbage trucks cruised Memphis streets under police escorts. Loeb maintained that the strike was illegal, so he would be breaking the law to negotiate. He said he wouldn't talk until strikers returned to work. But the men refused to work until Loeb recognized their union. Loeb insisted that national union leaders had provoked workers to strike and that the mayor understood worker needs better than these so-called outside agitators. Employees didn't need a union, and he wouldn't help them build one by approving dues checkoff—voluntary payroll contributions to a union fund. Union negotiators insisted on the dues checkoff and such other terms as a written contract, the development of formal procedures for addressing worker grievances, pay increases, the end of discriminatory promotion policies, and worker benefits such as pensions and health care.

Loeb refused to budge. The white press and public applauded his toughness, and he bragged about receiving "bushel baskets" of supportive letters. "Henry, I don't think you were elected to count letters," suggested city council member Lewis Donelson, who was white, on February 22 as Fred Davis's committee tried to settle the strike. "I do know how the white people feel, but you're the mayor of the other 40 percent, too." Such logic did not resonate with Loeb, perhaps because blacks hadn't voted for him. Whites had. He broke off communication with Jerry Wurf that same day. Six weeks would pass before the two would meet again.

On March 5, nearly 500 striking workers and supporters marched to city hall and interrupted the weekly city council meeting. The group hoped to break the strike deadlock with an escalating use of nonviolence. Gesturing to the 200 police officers watching over the capacity crowd, Lawson warned, "We will sit in this council room until you get a settlement or until they put us out." White council members hastened to adjourn the meeting and cut off the microphones. Only the three black councillors, joined by an increasingly sympathetic white member named Jerred Blanchard, stayed behind. Blanchard's supportive behavior earned him threats and slander.

Critics called him the council's "fourth *nigger,*" a slanderous corruption of the era's descriptive term for African Americans, *Negro.*

"We want jail, we want jail!" shouted the protesters as organizers and police authorities debated how to proceed. Eventually 121 people volunteered for arrest. They left the council chamber singing, paired two to each arresting officer. Young people waiting outside divided into the parallel lines of an honor guard; they touched the marchers' hands, cheered, and wept as workers and ministers, blacks and whites, men and women, all marched between their ranks toward

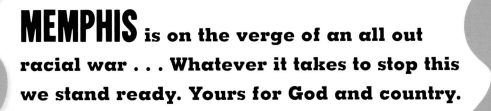

MEMPHIS is on the verge of an all out racial war . . . Whatever it takes to stop this we stand ready. Yours for God and country.

Telegram sent to city police on Tuesday, March 5 by a leader of the Tennessee Ku Klux Klan

jail. Protesters gained release within hours, some heading straight to that night's mass meeting.

Other actions of civil disobedience followed. Protesters staged pickets at garbage-truck barns. Some blocked truck trash routes (and were arrested). In a sign of increasing youth involvement, groups of teens started cutting school to march downtown and to city hall. Others began weekend pickets at suburban shopping malls. Strike supporters of all ages turned out on March 14 for the walkout's largest rally yet. Some 9,000 people gathered in Mason Temple to hear two of the nation's most prominent African-American leaders: Bayard Rustin, noted civil rights organizer, and Roy Wilkins, national president of the NAACP. "It's hard for whites to change their minds, even the good ones," joked Wilkins that night. He added, "And the bad ones just get worse."

Within days, news spread that the nation's most prominent advocate for civil rights was headed to Memphis. Martin Luther King, Jr., intended to add his support to the strike.

Chapter 4

A WAR ON POVERTY

"How can you get rid of poverty if working men don't get decent wages?" demanded Bayard Rustin when he spoke in Memphis on March 14, 1968. "If you can't get a decent salary for men who are working, in the name of God, how the hell are you gonna get rid of poverty?"

Rustin's cry echoed the passion of his colleague and friend Martin Luther King, Jr. All spring, as blacks fought for worker rights in Memphis, King struggled to launch his most ambitious civil rights effort yet: the Poor People's Campaign. The idea had started with a young lawyer and movement activist named Marian Wright. During April 1967 she had led a group of U.S. senators, including Robert F. Kennedy, on a tour of rural Mississippi. Kennedy, shaken by the depth of poverty he witnessed, commented to Wright that other Congress members would only understand the need for action if they saw similar scenes.

> **I asked my brother to come with me.**
> **I asked my brother to come with me.**
> **I asked my brother to come with me.**
> **I'm on my way, great God, I'm on my way.**
>
> *Verse from "I'm on My Way," a traditional spiritual*

During the Great Depression, the U.S. government documented the living conditions of the working poor. Photographers such as Dorothea Lange (above, her scene of a Mississippi cotton plantation, 1937) and Walker Evans (left, with rural residents in Alabama, 1936) captured conditions that persisted decades later.

When Wright joined King's advisers for a planning session the following September, she returned to this theme. Rather than coaxing legislators out to see the poor, why not bring the poor to see them at the nation's capital? Lawmakers would no longer be able to dismiss stories of American poverty as exaggerated or false. Wright recalled similar campaigns from the 1930s, such as the bonus marches by veterans of World War I and a threatened march over racial discrimination during World War II. Both had resulted in federal action.

"I'm on fire about the thing," King said of Wright's idea later that fall. Masses of poor people could be mobilized in such nonviolent actions as marching, speeches, and a camp-in to assert their rights to economic justice. He saw the project as the culmination of his fight for human rights. If it succeeded, his work would be complete; if it failed, at least he would have tried. King knew that achieving what he called the Poor People's Campaign for Jobs or Income would be challenging. Poverty cut across all races and backgrounds, all regions and ages. Just mobilizing such a diverse population would be problematic; convincing lawmakers to support expensive legislation would be harder yet.

King asked members of his Southern Christian Leadership Conference staff to collaborate on the project, but few of his SCLC associates embraced the idea with King's enthusiasm. The concept was too ambitious, too broadly focused, too likely to fail, they argued. It required building connections across unfamiliar ethnic and geographic lines to Native Americans, Latinos, and poor whites. It would be a logistical nightmare—and expensive—to transport poor people to Washington, house them, and feed them. What would they do when they got there? How long would they stay? What if government officials reacted with resentment instead of sympathy?

Undeterred, King began promoting the idea in late 1967. By February 1968—during the same week when workers went on strike in Memphis—King was seeking money to support it. "We intend to channelize the smoldering rage of the Negro and white poor in an effective militant movement," he wrote in an SCLC fund-raising letter. "A pilgrimage of the poor will gather in Washington from the slums and the rural starvation regions of the nation. We will go there, and we will demand to be heard, and we will stay until America responds."

In 1932 impoverished veterans of World War I marched in Washington, D.C. (right), advocating for prepayment of their combat retirement bonuses. The so-called bonus marchers settled into camps (below, a vet with his family). When President Herbert Hoover ordered them evicted, federal troops did so with tanks, tear gas, a cavalry charge, and brute force. Protesters returned yearly until Congress met their demands in 1936.

President Johnson shared King's interest in ending poverty; he'd even declared what he called the War on Poverty. But Johnson had expended much of his political influence through the passage of other landmark civil rights legislation, and his support of an increasingly controversial and costly war in Vietnam meant that funds were short for new

After the Kerner Commission report on urban violence appeared in early March, King used the findings to support the need for his campaign. President Lyndon B. Johnson had asked the commission to evaluate the causes of recent race riots in major U.S. cities. Instead of showing that rebellious citizens had provoked the riots, as many people had suggested, the commission affirmed the politically less popular interpretation suggested by King: Poverty, unemployment, and racial tensions had fed the violence. In order to avoid further unrest, the report stated, the government would need to reduce poverty.

President Johnson shared King's interest in ending poverty; he'd even declared what he called the War on Poverty. But Johnson had expended much of his political influence through the passage of other landmark civil rights legislation, and his support of an increasingly controversial and costly war in Vietnam meant that funds were short for new domestic programs. So were friends. Antiwar Democrats were challenging the President's right to represent their party in the 1968 presidential election. After King began criticizing the Vietnam War in 1967, Johnson distanced himself from his civil rights ally.

J. Edgar Hoover, director of the Federal Bureau of Investigation (FBI), harbored an intense dislike of King, fueled in part by his rejection of the civil rights leader's vision for social change. The FBI had spied on King for years, at Hoover's insistence. In 1968 Hoover overstepped the bounds of law and launched operation POCAM, a systematic attempt to undermine the Poor People Campaign. FBI agents hired informants, planted false news stories, and paid critics to spread bogus rumors about the campaign. Such reports warned that participants would lose welfare support, be poorly cared for in the nation's capital, and become stranded when the rally ended. No lesser a figure than the SCLC finance manager became an FBI spy. "No opportunity should be missed," directed Hoover, "to insure the targeted group is disrupted, ridiculed, or discredited."

FBI efforts complicated King's ability to raise money and his staff's success at recruiting participants. By early March — as Memphis workers and supporters prepared to go to jail — King had to announce a delayed start for the effort. Undeterred, and unaware of the FBI's sabotage, King persevered. In an attempt to motivate his staff, he "preached like a salmon fighting upstream," observed King biographer Taylor Branch. Trusted associate Andrew Young joked that his boss maintained a "war on sleep" in his efforts to wage a war on poverty.

King crisscrossed the nation to speak to donors, address crowds of supporters, and attend SCLC planning meetings. Aides such as Young, Ralph D. Abernathy, Jesse Jackson, Jr., and Bernard Lee struggled to match his pace.

When James Lawson caught up with King by phone to invite him to speak in Memphis, aides protested that the stop would divert King from touring Mississippi and Alabama to recruit campaign participants. But King recognized that striking Memphis workers represented exactly the sort of poor people his effort sought to help. He could make an overnight stop in Memphis and head south across the border into Mississippi without delaying his recruitment trip. King agreed to go.

The Memphis strike entered its sixth week as King approached the city on Monday, March 18, 1968. Police continued to target blacks for random harassment. Vandals had begun setting uncollected garbage on fire. Scab laborers enabled almost half the city's garbage trucks to function. Fatigue spread among strikers and their supporters. Even as the *Commercial Appeal* encouraged the city council to end the stalemate, and whites began questioning the mayor's rigid stance, he held his ground. When a group of white women suggested compromise, Henry Loeb told one of them, a graduate of England's prestigious Oxford University, "Well, you're sweet and you're a pretty little thing, but you just don't know what you're talking about." Union leader Jerry Wurf described his unusual role in Memphis: "The goddamned mayor was pouring gasoline on the situation and I ran around pulling matches out of people's hands."

Lawson welcomed King to Memphis on Monday evening with a report that earlier crowd predictions of 10,000 people might be in doubt. A flash of disappointment crossed King's face. Then union rep Jesse Epps, acting as Lawson's sidekick in their prearranged joke, added that at least 15,000 people awaited him: "No one else can get in the house." As Lawson recalled, King "just lit up like a lantern." A team of advance men had to part the crowd at Mason Temple so King could join the in-progress meeting.

"All labor has dignity," he told the welcoming crowd. "You are reminding not only Memphis, but you are reminding the nation that it is a crime for people to live in this rich nation and receive starvation wages." King spoke for more than an hour, encouraging those assembled to stick to their goals "so that you will be able to make Mayor Loeb and others say 'Yes' even when they want to say 'No.'" He reminded them, "Freedom is not something that is voluntarily given by the oppressor . . . It is something that must be demanded by the oppressed . . . If we are going to get equality, if we are going to get adequate wages, we are going to have to struggle for it."

Then King paused and offered a spontaneous suggestion that electrified the hall. "You know what?" he asked. "You may have to escalate the struggle a bit," he suggested. "In a few days you ought to get together and just have a general work

I'M NOT only concerned about the black poor. I'm concerned about the white poor. I'm concerned about the Puerto Rican poor, the Indian poor. I'm concerned about the Mexican-American poor. We are going to grapple with the problem of poor people . . . black and white together.

Martin Luther King, Jr., speaking on February 15, 1968, in Birmingham, Alabama

stoppage in the city of Memphis!" Spectators cheered and leaped to their feet. They were thrilled by the idea of crippling Memphis with a loss of the services provided by African Americans—ranging from teachers to household help to factory workers to other city employees. King, his traveling aides, and strike organizers made a spontaneous decision: He would return to Memphis later that week and lead the absentee workers on a march through downtown.

Suddenly the poor people of Memphis represented the heart of King's Poor People's Campaign, and King represented the force needed to take the Memphis strike to victory.

Chapter 5

MARCHING
IN MEMPHIS

"There are no masses in this mass movement," Martin Luther King, Jr., had observed about the Poor People's Campaign in February 1968.

Thus King's spirits had soared when he visited Memphis and found exactly the energy, individuals, and purpose he'd been seeking. He checked out of the local Lorraine Motel on March 19 with renewed hope that the city's labor struggle would inspire his own work. By the time he reached his home in Atlanta two days later, though, King was sobered, exhausted, and discouraged all over again. The deprivation he'd seen in rural Mississippi and Alabama literally had made him cry. Organizing such bone-poor folks seemed impossible. In the course of a week he'd made 35 speeches, but the campaign still hadn't gelled.

Would you have freedom from wage slavery? Then join in the grand Industrial band; Would you from misery and hunger be free? Then come do your share like a man.

Verse from "There Is Power in a Union,"
one of the popular anthems during labor
struggles at the turn of the 20th century

Clayborn Temple (left) served
as a hub for 1968 strike activity.
The daily picketers' walk from
there to city hall covered 1.3
miles. Violence escalated
on March 28 as police pulled
over motorists (pictured here),
attacking at random or with
purpose—for example, breaking out the windows on a truck
because it sheltered union
organizer P. J. Ciampa.

**n unlikely southern snowstorm** put an end to King's anticipated return to Memphis on March 22. James Lawson called King before dawn that Friday to report that his city lay paralyzed under a 16-inch blanket of snow. There would be no march. "We've got the perfect work stoppage, though!" he joked. Reluctantly, everyone rescheduled the event for March 28, and King renewed his war on sleep with more travel, preaching, fund-raising speeches, and late-night planning sessions.

In Memphis, the spring snow vanished as quickly as it had arrived, and picket marches resumed. With no end in sight for the strike, Lawson and other COME organizers conserved movement energy by reducing mass meetings from nightly to three times a week. T. O. Jones, P. J. Ciampa, and other union organizers continued meeting daily with striking workers, even as Public Works Director Charles Blackburn focused his efforts on managing the makeshift collection of the city's garbage.

King's visit had raised the strike's profile, at least, and much needed financial support arrived from distant unions. Even more important, King's high-profile support prompted local leaders to soften their refusal to negotiate. With the secret blessing of Henry Loeb, the city council approved a plan to hold talks with labor representatives mediated by local negotiator Frank Miles. AFSCME officials in Memphis jumped at the chance to renew negotiations. The talks collapsed within days, though, because the mayor violated the agreed-upon ground rules of participating in meetings but remaining silent about negotiations to news reporters.

Meanwhile, FBI agents and Memphis police swapped tips that they gathered from informants, and overworked local law enforcement officers (most now working seven days a week) manned the front lines of an increasingly tense, racially charged street scene. Hundreds of local youths now supported the strike. Most were African-American teens, including an uncertain number allied with a group called the Black Organizing Project, or BOP, and a loose offshoot named for a popular television show about space aliens, the Invaders. Many of these younger activists felt discouraged by the persistence of poverty, unemployment,

On March 22, 1968, a Detroit union autoworker (above) trudged through the snow to honor the day's original plan for marching to city hall. Mayor Henry Loeb, who had managed to get to work, offered him coffee. A local sent the mayor a letter crediting God's hand in stopping the march. The writer, who signed the letter as "a tax payer,"

and prejudice despite nonviolent campaigns for change. They drew inspiration from the nation's rising Black Power movement. No longer was it "considered a noble deed, man, to lay down in the street and let some cat beat you up," suggested Memphis Invader Calvin Taylor.

Local youths, wearing jackets emblazoned with the name Invaders, began calling for physical retaliation against white oppression. Such expressions concerned COME ministers, AFSCME union leaders, and others, especially because BOP's youthful organizers seemed to have little control over their followers. Adults worried that the FBI or others might have infiltrated these groups to spy or to incite misbehavior that would disrupt and discredit the

"THOSE damn kids. Between the kids and the cops the whole town's going to blow up.

Unidentified African-American woman after seeking shelter at Clayborn Temple on March 28, 1968

works of more moderate organizations. Indeed, the police had planted at least one officer among the Invaders—Agent 500. This African-American Vietnam veteran, working under the cover name Max McCullough, quickly rose to influence as BOP's so-called minister of transportation because he owned a car.

"The only force we will use is soul-force which is peaceful, loving, courageous, yet militant," COME organizers had emphasized as they promoted the rescheduled mass march. Enthusiastic participants began gathering two hours early on Thursday, March 28. By the scheduled start time of 10 a.m., as many as 15,000 or more people had assembled outside Clayborn Temple on a rapidly warming day. Some 1,000 striking workers prepared to lead the procession. Hundreds of them hoisted large cardboard placards bearing four words—I AM A MAN—with *am* underlined for emphasis. They were joined by wives, children, other relatives, neighbors, ministers (even a few white clergy members), more than a dozen white nuns, African-American schoolteachers who dared to visibly support the strike, white and black college students, white trade union representatives, and others.

Students turned out in response to COME flyers written with such slang-filled lines as, "If your school is tops, Pops, prove it!" and "Together we stick, divided we're stuck, Baby." The festive mood of the gathering began to fray as students started arriving with ominous reports of an early morning skirmish between young people and police at mostly black Hamilton High School. A girl had been taken to the hospital in an ambulance; perhaps the police had killed her. (They hadn't.)

A rougher element began to infiltrate the gathering, too. Young people wearing Invader-labeled jackets arrived. Others carried homemade signs addressing the mayor with profanity. Some young men stripped the handles from official protest signs and grasped the four-foot-long wooden sticks like clubs. Local drunks and pickpockets milled about. A group of men broke into a neighboring liquor store. Parade marshals sought to weed out troublemakers, but the size of the crowd overwhelmed them. A modest police detail of 350 officers hovered out of sight, a tactic that prevented racially charged confrontations from occurring between officers and spectators but created an unsupervised, free-for-all atmosphere.

Tempers flared in the restless crowd as the day grew hot and the march failed to start. King's war on sleep and overcommitted schedule found him running late that morning, bound for Memphis aboard a delayed flight. When he reached downtown, crowds engulfed his vehicle, creating further delays. King and other leaders finally locked arms and stepped off toward city hall more than an hour behind schedule. Striking workers followed, holding aloft their I <u>AM</u> A MAN signs as the group proceeded north from Clayborn Temple to Beale Street. Marchers progressed past several blocks of movie theaters, blues clubs, retail stores, and pawn shops.

Yet experienced participants knew the event did not feel right. Young people crowded their way forward. King, fatigued and practically carried along by those who grasped his arms, complained that the crowds were pushing him. Others observed that their heels were being trampled. So far they'd traveled about seven blocks and were almost halfway toward the destination of city hall. Not even 15 minutes had elapsed since the start of the march.

As the group turned right to begin the gentle climb up Main Street, ominous sounds echoed from behind the front ranks. Vandals along Beale Street had begun beating on the thick plate-glass storefront windows with placard sticks and scavenged metal pipes. Glass shattered in the wake of the marchers even as troublemakers raced to attack the windows that lay ahead.

By the scheduled start time of 10 a.m., as many as 15,000 or more people had assembled outside Clayborn Temple on a rapidly warming day. Some 1,000 striking workers prepared to lead the procession. Hundreds of them hoisted large cardboard placards bearing four words— I AM A MAN—with *am* underlined for emphasis.

On March 28, 1968, striking workers massed in a show of nonviolent protest (above) for a march with Martin Luther King, Jr. Young people allied with the Invaders felt they offered a counterweight to the emphasis King and local organizer James Lawson placed on nonviolent action. "We were representing the threats that Lawson and them would need in order to sort of make the white man afraid," suggested Calvin Taylor. Such fears, the Invaders believed, would force the establishment to settle the strike. When violence disrupted the March 28 event, participants fled in disarray (left).

Police officers formed a line across Main Street, signaling that the march could not continue. Lawson borrowed a police bullhorn so he could be heard over the tumult as he advised marchers to turn around and return to Clayborn Temple.

Organizers feared for King's safety and urged him to leave the scene. At first he resisted, arguing with Lawson, "Jim, they'll say I ran away." Others persisted until King agreed, "I've got to get out of here." King's traveling aide, Bernard Lee, flagged down a car and convinced its two African-American female occupants to let him drive while King, his SCLC partner Ralph Abernathy, and two others crowded into the back. Lee recruited a motorcycle cop to help clear their path and escort them to shelter. Crowds cut off access to the upscale Peabody Hotel and to the Lorraine, the black-owned motel where King had stayed earlier that month, so the officer escorted them to the local Holiday Inn, a high-rise that offered the added security of interior corridors. Safely in a hotel room, a horrified King watched televised news reports of the mayhem that followed his departure.

Criminal elements in the crowd took advantage of the chaos and began stealing merchandise from the broken windows while young people expressed their accumulated frustration by breaking more glass. Brawls broke out between police officers and the vandals in an explosion of racially laced tensions that had built for weeks—and lifetimes. Young males launched rocks and bottles at the police. Policemen retaliated with Mace and tear gas–filled grenades. Officers swore and yelled insults as they beat peaceful marchers and aggressive youths alike. They layered blows on some victims until they collapsed, unconscious, and landed single whacks on others unfortunate enough to be within arm's reach. They also attacked members of the media, who tried to document a scene that looked to one reporter "like a battlefield."

Parade marshals struggled to direct nonviolent march participants through the tear gas and confusion toward the sanctuary of Clayborn Temple. Once there, able-bodied survivors helped others treat the symptoms of tear gas, find lost family members, and tend to wounds. Yet almost immediately, fighting engulfed this refuge. Young men massed inside and outside the stone building as if defending a fortress. Police attempted to dislodge them with tear gas, adding to the misery of as many as 2,000 marchers sheltered inside. More than a dozen officers stormed the church, firing more tear gas and clubbing people indiscriminately. Some scared occupants literally jumped out of windows in an attempt to escape. As late as 2 p.m.—some three hours after the delayed start of the march—police continued to attack those trying to flee Clayborn Temple.

Meanwhile, roaming groups of officers vented

their pent-up fury by raiding popular African-American gathering spots. Unprovoked, they clubbed patrons and broke car windshields of those who fled. Carloads of officers responded to a prank fire alarm at Booker T. Washington High School by attacking students and staff with tear gas and clubs. Elsewhere, 16-year-old Larry Payne, who was black, found himself cornered by police, perhaps caught in the act of stealing from a vandalized store. Eyewitnesses claimed Payne stood weaponless, hands raised, pleading for his life, as a white policeman held a sawed-off shotgun to his abdomen. The officer fired, asserting later that Payne had threatened him with a knife.

Payne was the day's sole fatality. Sixty blacks required hospitalization; countless suffered less serious wounds. Nine policemen received medical care. By the end of the day, police had arrested more than 500 people ranging in age from 12 to 75. Most were young black males. The mayor imposed a 7 p.m. curfew on the city, and Tennessee legislators declared a state of emergency there. By nightfall, a force of nearly 4,000 predominantly white National Guard soldiers cruised the streets of Memphis in troop trucks and tanks, with bayonets affixed to their rifles.

Late in the afternoon Martin Luther King, Jr., emerged from his hotel room to join a press conference with strike organizers. The group tried to focus media attention on the underlying causes of the day's violence, not the violence itself, and to urge resolution of the labor strike. "We are now saying to the city, 'Will you please listen?'" said James Lawson. "'Will you please recognize that in the heart of your city there is massive cruelty and poverty and indignity, and that only if you remove it can we have order.'" Then, miserable, King returned to his room. "Maybe we just have to give up and let violence take its course," he told Ralph Abernathy and Bernard Lee. So many people had been injured. Larry Payne lay dead. The Memphis movement had stalled. King's reputation, the cause of nonviolence, and the fate of the Poor People's Campaign all seemed in jeopardy.

Just ten days earlier, Memphis had lifted King's spirits by illuminating a path for helping America's poorest citizens. Now, in Memphis, King felt only despair.

Chapter 6

LAST DAYS

"I had never seen him in all my life so upset and so troubled," recalled Ralph Abernathy, childhood friend and closest colleague of Martin Luther King, Jr. The distressed civil rights leader stayed up until dawn after the failed Memphis protest on March 28. "He was worried, worried," said Abernathy. "He didn't know what to do."

Throughout King's restless night, National Guard troops enforced a state of emergency on Memphis that would last for the next five days. Police patrolled the streets, as well, and systematically harassed members of the African-American community. The city's black youth limited most of its retaliation to the pulling of false fire alarms. No one else died. Many credited the strike's emphasis on nonviolence with keeping the city from exploding into the sort of extended riots that had occurred in earlier years in such places as Los Angeles and Detroit.

> **Ain't gonna let nobody turn me round,**
> **Turn me round, turn me round.**
> **Ain't gonna let nobody turn me round—**
> **I'm gonna keep on a-walkin', keep on a-talkin',**
> **Marching up to freedom land.**

From a traditional spiritual adapted into
a freedom song during the civil rights movement

Tanks and armed soldiers
shared the streets of Memphis
with protesters (left) following
the riot of March 28. Even in
his despair over the situation,
Martin Luther King, Jr., personified
his commitment to nonviolence.
After meeting King on March 29,
the Invader Calvin Taylor
observed, "Nobody could be as
peaceful as that man," adding,
"It was one of the few times in
my life when I wasn't actually
fighting something."

**resident Lyndon B. Johnson condemned** the lawlessness in Memphis and offered to send a federal mediator to help settle the strike. Mayor Henry Loeb refused the help. Alarmed members of the city council grew weary with the mayor's unyielding stubbornness, and the day following the riot three whites joined the council's three blacks in support of a resolution to end the strike—one member shy of the majority required for action.

Withering media coverage awaited King when he awoke on Friday. Commentators noted how the champion of nonviolence had led a rioting mob through Memphis. The *Commercial Appeal* borrowed the name of a popular recipe to dub him Chicken a la King for fleeing the scene. Politicians and reporters wondered: If King could not lead a peaceful march in Memphis, how could he possibly control an invasion of Washington, D.C., by the nation's poor?

Everyone asked: What went wrong on Friday? Who was to blame for the failed march? King? Poor planning? The Invaders? Opportunistic thieves? Mischief makers intent on sabotaging the event? Had police officers made matters worse with their violent pushback, or had they prevented an even larger riot from unfolding? James Lawson and other COME organizers scanned photos of Thursday's crowd for familiar faces. They concluded that the leaders of the Invaders had not been present to orchestrate the disturbance, which confirmed the group's pleas of innocence. "We don't have to organize," observed Coby Smith in a Friday interview. "The police beat heads—they organize for us." Could the root cause of the violence be poverty and racial oppression, as King, Lawson, and others asserted? The questions looped into an unsolved riddle of cause and effect.

"What must be done to have a peaceful march?" King asked three leaders of the Invaders who unexpectedly knocked on his hotel room door Friday morning. "You know I have got to lead one. There is no other way." King knew that in order to revive his dream of a Poor People's Campaign, he would have to lead a successful march in Memphis. Lawson wanted to attempt the effort the next day. King and his advisers insisted on a delay for more planning, though, and they left town.

"The boy looked so innocent," community leader Maxine Smith recalled about the visitation held for Larry Payne in early April (above). The role the youth played in looting remained unclear (at left, wearing a white shirt, hours before his death), as did the circumstances of his death. No charges were ever filed against the officer who shot him, in part because police had dumped evidence from the shooting in the nearby Mississippi River.

On Saturday, March 30, King met for hours in Atlanta with core leaders from the SCLC. They argued and complained, disagreeing on the merits of the Memphis diversion, the fate of the Poor People's Campaign, and what to do next. Finally, an exasperated King shocked the group by rebuking them and walking out. The stunned staffers caught their breaths and then rallied on their own around King's agenda. They would send an advance team to help lead workshops on nonviolence in Memphis, and they would top off a successful march there with a full-force campaign in Washington, D.C. Within days, everyone had settled on a date for the Memphis mass march: April 8.

When King preached on March 31 at the National Cathedral in Washington, D.C., he recalled a biblical story that he had cited during other recent speeches, too. He reminded those gathered of Lazarus, the poor man who had gone to heaven while Dives, a local rich man, had not. "Dives went to hell because he passed Lazarus every day but he never really saw him," King had explained in Birmingham in February. "If America does not use her vast resources to end poverty and make it possible for all of God's children to have the basic necessities of life, *she too is going to hell,*" King had warned in Memphis. As King spoke that last Sunday in March to some 4,000 people gathered in the nation's capital, he reminded them of the shared responsibility people had to care for the poor. He proclaimed, "We are coming to Washington in a 'poor people's campaign.'" No solution to the nation's poverty would occur, he challenged the assembly, "'til people of good will put their hearts and souls in motion."

Three days later, King returned to Memphis on another delayed flight; this time a bomb threat directed at the civil rights leader had caused a time-consuming search of the plane. A handful of SCLC aides accompanied King, including the FBI's informant who was tasked with passing along insider news while in Memphis. "Either the Movement lives or dies in Memphis," King told union organizer Jesse Epps after the flight landed safely.

Security for King proved problematic in Memphis. Based on his nonviolent principles, King traveled without armed protection, and it seemed clear that surveillance, not King's security, lay behind offers of police protection in Memphis. A pair of undercover African-American officers began tailing King's group as they headed to an organizational meeting at James Lawson's church.

This and other surveillance persisted after the travelers checked in to the Lorraine Motel. The choice of the Lorraine made political sense — King had stayed there before, and he had been criticized after the March 28 riot for fleeing to the fashionable, historically white Holiday Inn instead of the more modest and historically black Lorraine. But the Lorraine's design represented a security risk; its exterior corridors meant King's whereabouts and movements around the property were visible.

A major spring storm advanced on Memphis as King attended afternoon meetings and settled in to his hotel room. By evening not just thunder and lightning but high winds and tornadoes threatened the region. Nonetheless, 2,000 to 3,000 hardy souls braved the weather to gather at Mason Temple

IT IS in your power to mold Memphis into a genuine city, or to reduce it to a pile of stinking rubble. May history praise you as a man of wisdom—not condemn you as a fool.

Carroll Richards, a Memphis white, from a published letter to the mayor, March 1968

in anticipation of hearing another speech by King. Not feeling well, and concerned that the media would blame him instead of the storm for the small turnout, King asked Ralph Abernathy to speak for him instead. But when Abernathy reached the hall, he called King and urged him to come after all. True, the March 18 crowd dwarfed this small assembly, but these folks had just about risked their lives to gather, and they deserved to hear King himself. King rallied and earned a standing ovation when he arrived about 9 p.m. Abernathy delivered a long personal introduction that some ministers teasingly compared to the sort of tribute one would hear at a funeral. Then King began to speak.

Politicians and reporters wondered: If King could not lead a peaceful march in Memphis, how could he possibly control an invasio of Washington, D.C., by the nation's poor? Everyone asked: What went wrong?

"Ain't we gonna march today?" asked a sanitation worker on Friday, March 29, after union officials hesitated to resume the regular pickets in the aftermath of the previous day's violence. That afternoon as many as 300 men assembled at Clayborn Temple, shook hands with a supportive minister, and marched single file into city hall and back under the tense scrutiny of local police, National Guardsmen, and shotgun-armed storekeepers.

Without any notes or script, the gifted orator threaded together new material with excerpts from oft-delivered remarks. He talked about the parable of the Good Samaritan, the biblical figure who helps the victim of a robbery along the dangerous road between Jerusalem and Jericho. King speculated that earlier passersby had not stopped to help the injured man because they may have worried they could be robbed, too. The Good Samaritan, in contrast, apparently worried more about the victim's safety than his own. A similar sense of self-sacrifice empowers the Memphis movement, too, King observed.

WE'VE GOT TO give ourselves to this struggle until the end. Nothing could be more tragic than to stop at this point, in Memphis. We've got to see it through . . . Be concerned about your brother. You may not be on strike. But either we go up together or we go down together.

Martin Luther King, Jr., April 3, 1968

Then King reminded the audience how a mentally ill woman had stabbed him years earlier in New York City. He later learned that, had he sneezed before doctors could remove the weapon, he would have died. King observed how glad he was that he had not sneezed, for, if he had, he would have missed all the momentous events that had followed in the civil rights movement. "If I had sneezed," he added, "I wouldn't have been in Memphis to see the community rally around those brothers and sisters who are suffering. I'm so happy that I didn't sneeze."

An electric air hung over the audience as King's voice competed with the sounds of the storm raging outside. Experienced preachers seated on stage behind him wondered how he would be able to close his remarks. Each new oratorical flourish seemed to top the one before it. Could he soar higher yet?

Looking off into the distance, King revealed how his life had been threatened during his morning flight to Memphis. What future risks might he face from "our sick white brothers?" Then he jolted ministers and audience alike with a stunning finale.

"Like anybody," he said, "I would like to live a long life. Longevity has its place." But, said King, his focus was on the needs of the moment, not his life span. Referencing the Bible as he built toward his conclusion, he evoked the familiar story of Moses leading his followers toward land that God had promised them. Moses reaches a mountaintop from which he can see the land spread out before him, but he dies before his group can reach its destination. King proclaimed that God had allowed him, as with Moses, "to go up to the mountain. And I've looked over. And I've seen the promised land," he announced, drawing out the vowels in the word *seen* as if to emphasize that he had surveyed a vast space.

"I may not get there with you," King observed with visible emotion. "But I want you to know tonight, that we, as a people, will get to the promised land." The audience responded with roaring affirmation of his message as he reassured the crowd, "I'm happy, tonight. I'm not worried about anything. I'm not fearing any man." Blinking back tears, he turned toward his colleagues behind him and concluded, "Mine eyes have seen the glory of the coming of the Lord."

Commotion engulfed the crowd. Cheers drowned out all sounds from the evening's storm. Many people leaped to their feet, shouted, and clapped their hands. Others sat sobbing, consumed with emotion. Ministers wept, too, as they embraced King and marveled at his speaking prowess. Workers and other strike supporters mingled with King and strike organizers. As people drifted away from Mason Temple, they walked under unexpectedly calm skies, and their excitement from the remarkable speech mellowed into a satisfying confidence about what lay ahead.

"There was an overcoming mood, an overcoming spirit in that place," recalled one local minister. "When Dr. King spoke that night we knew that we were going to win."

Chapter 7

DEATH IN
MEMPHIS, REPRISE

"I'd rather be dead than afraid," Martin Luther King, Jr.,
told members of his staff on the afternoon of April 4. "You've
got to get over being afraid of death," he said.

King, his colleagues, and his family had all known for years
that his nonviolent activism triggered violent responses from
those who felt threatened by social change. People had bombed
his home in 1956 during the Montgomery bus boycott, physically
attacked him on more than one occasion, and threatened him
countless others. As early as 1963, following the assassination
of President John F. Kennedy, King had predicted to his wife
Coretta Scott King, "This is what is going to happen to me."

Such worries, even premonitions of his death, intensified
during 1968, both among those around him and for King himself.
During a February 4 sermon he suggested how to remember
him at his funeral:

> **"Oh, freedom, oh, freedom, oh freedom over me,
> And before I'll be a slave, I'll be buried in my grave,
> And I'll fight for the right to be free.**

From a traditional spiritual adapted into a freedom song during the civil rights movement

During his April 3 speech at Mason Temple (left), Martin Luther King, Jr., promised to challenge the day's court order that prohibited him from marching on April 8. He pledged to participate regardless of whether or not the court sided with him or with Henry Loeb (above, left, on April 3, outside the federal courthouse). King playfully suggested in his remarks that "Mayor Loeb is in dire need of a doctor."

**S**ay that I was a drum major for justice; say that I was a drum major for peace; I was a drum major for righteousness," he proposed at the time. In late March, when a friend questioned his lack of personal security, King replied, "If they couldn't protect Kennedy, how can they protect me?" Before he left for his April trip to Memphis, King warned his wife and parents that he could be killed at any time. "Martin didn't say directly to me that it's going to happen in Memphis," Coretta Scott King later recalled, "but I think he felt that time was running out." Many who heard King speak during the stormy night of April 3 found their enthusiasm for his powerful message tempered by an uneasy sense that King had just foretold his own death.

Yet King seemed lighthearted and carefree after the speech. He spent the rest of that evening with friends and celebrated the late-night arrival of his brother A. D. King at the Lorraine. On April 4 he remained at the motel, holding a staff meeting in his room, talking again with members of the Invaders, and taking time to relax. King hung out with his brother. The pair phoned their parents for an extended chat, at times teasing their mother about which one of her sons was speaking. For lunch King and Ralph Abernathy shared a catfish meal in their room, number 306. In anticipation of a supper party, the friends phoned the event's hostess and quizzed her about the ample menu.

Evening plans called for everyone to gather after this early meal for a mass meeting at Mason Temple. The program called for, among other events, another speech by King and a performance by the Operation Breadbasket Band, a group directed by King's SCLC colleague Jesse Jackson. At one point during the afternoon, members of the Chicago-based group gathered informally in a motel room and sang church music and freedom songs for King and others. King exclaimed later to a local preacher that the spirit in Memphis felt just "like the old Movement days."

Unbeknownst to those at the Lorraine Motel, a pair of African-American undercover policemen watched all of these comings and goings from an observation point across Mulberry Street, the modest thoroughfare in front of the motel. They worked from inside a neighborhood fire station, where they took turns peering with binoculars through a small hole cut into a layer of newspaper placed over a window. Someone else began watching King that afternoon, too. James

As the civil rights movement broke through social justice barriers with integration and increased voting rights, Martin Luther King, Jr., increasingly emphasized such economic justice themes as jobs, improved working conditions, and fair wages. King lived on the go in the company of SCLC staffers (above, King arriving in Memphis on April 3 with, from left, Andrew Young, Ralph Abernathy, and Bernard Lee).

Earl Ray, an escaped white convict traveling under an assumed name, had just rented a room in a boardinghouse next door to the fire station. He'd chosen the establishment because it overlooked the location of someone he'd begun to stalk in recent weeks, someone he wanted to kill. Someone named Martin Luther King, Jr.

Late in the afternoon Andrew Young arrived at the Lorraine to report on his daylong appearance at a court hearing related to the April 8 march. City officials had asked a local judge to prohibit King and other SCLC staffers from organizing and participating in the event. Their involvement might trigger more violence, warned Mayor Henry Loeb in the city's request. The judge had initially sided with the city and issued an injunction of restraint. The day's hearing allowed for further consideration of the matter.

I WOULD LIKE to remind you that there is no place else in the world where people even assume that this kind of change should come about nonviolently except Martin Luther King and the Southern Christian Leadership Conference.

Andrew Young, testifying on April 3, 1968, for the right to march in Memphis

When Young arrived, King playfully pounced on him, pulled him to the floor, and started to tickle him. Others joined in, scolding Young for not providing reports throughout the day. The tickling progressed into a spirited pillow fight with King, his brother, Young, and several others. Soon after the silliness ended, one of their lawyers arrived to announce that the judge had lifted his restrictions: The march could proceed as planned. In top spirits, King and the others returned to their rooms to get ready for dinner.

Shortly before 6 p.m., officer Willie Richmond observed King emerging from his room. While others finished their preparations, King lingered at the adjacent balcony railing and visited with those already outside. He joked as several SCLC staffers pretended to roughhouse in the parking lot. Marrell "Max" McCullough, the undercover cop posing as an Invader, stood nearby; as the group's so-called minister of transportation, he and his blue Volkswagen had become useful to the out-of-towners. King's own volunteer driver, Solomon Jones, waited below, too, with a borrowed white Cadillac. One minute, two minutes ticked by while the group prepared to depart.

James Earl Ray watched from his bedroom through binoculars as the scene began to unfold across Mulberry Street, some 70 yards away. A recently purchased Remington rifle rested nearby. Ray had realized after renting the room that he would only be able to fire his gun by leaning out of the bedroom window and aiming around a building setback. Such a maneuver could easily have attracted attention, so Ray had investigated the nearby communal bathroom and discovered that a small window situated over the bathtub offered an unobstructed view of the Lorraine.

As King stood outside, Ray dashed to the bathroom, reconfirmed the superior sight lines, returned to his room, secured his weapon and miscellaneous belongings in an old bedspread, and rushed back to the vacant bathroom. Another minute, then perhaps one more passed, while King visited with friends, ducked briefly into his room, then returned to his balcony post. At one point Solomon Jones called up to suggest that King grab a coat; an evening chill was starting to develop, although the sun had not yet set. Having vacated his room, Ray locked the bathroom door, loaded one bullet in his gun, stepped into the tub, raised the bathroom window, and captured King in his rifle sight. The scope's magnification cut the appearance of the distance between the two men to 30 feet, making it easy for Ray to zoom in on his target.

For a few seconds, King struck up a conversation with Ben Branch, a singer and musician from the Breadbasket Band. King requested that Branch perform "Precious Lord, Take My Hand" during the group's presentation that night. Play it "like you've never played it before," King urged. Branch replied, "Dr. King, you know I do that all the time." King insisted, "But tonight, especially for me, I want you to play it real pretty."

Then Ray pulled the trigger. Almost instantaneously his bullet hit King in the throat with a destructive force designed to fell big game.

Having vacated his room, Ray locked the bathroom door, loaded one bullet in his gun, stepped into the tub, raised the bathroom window, and captured King in his rifle sight. The scope's magnification cut the appearance of the distance between the two men to 30 feet.

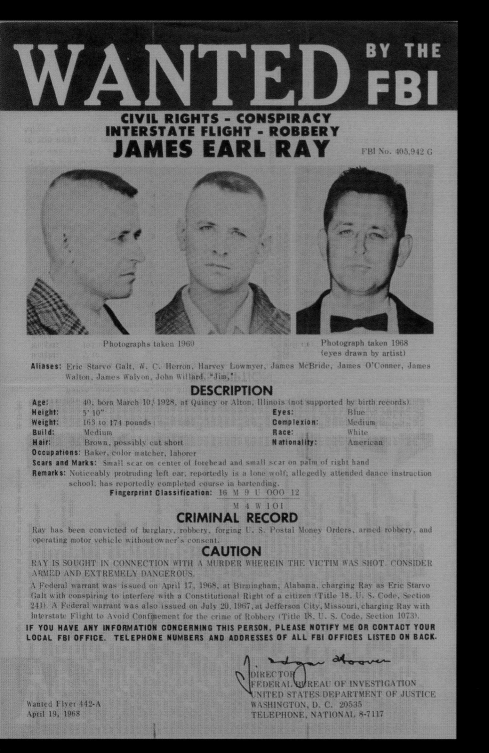

James Earl Ray was already wanted by the law before he assassinated Martin Luther King, Jr. (left, the previous evening, with Jesse Jackson). Ray had escaped from a Missouri prison almost a year earlier and concealed himself using a string of aliases—and even plastic surgery—prior to tracking King to Memphis. The FBI pieced together Ray's background (above) as he tried to flee to the African country of Zimbabwe, then known as white-supremacist Rhodesia.

Some said the gunshot sounded like a firecracker. Others thought a bomb had exploded or a vehicle had backfired. Reacting instinctively, many thought of gunfire and ducked behind cars, fearing other shots could follow. None did. Ray's sole target lay sprawled on a balcony, and the shooter had a new priority: to flee.

Undercover police officer McCullough reached King almost immediately. The civil rights icon was still alive, although blood poured from the right side of his neck and jaw. Using a small towel, McCullough applied pressure to the wound. Ralph Abernathy rushed forward with a larger towel. Someone else brought a bedspread. King's eyes were open, and he seemed to want to speak

WHERE'D THE shot come from? Where'd the shot come from?

Police officers arriving at the scene of the attack

but could not. People fumbled to call for an ambulance. Hotel co-owner Lorene Bailey, usually an accomplished operator of the motel's switchboard system for guest room telephones, went into shock and began muttering, nonsensically, "Somebody done hit that old white truck." Back in the parking lot, an unsettled Solomon Jones sat in the Cadillac and began repetitively driving the car forward, then reversing it. A. D. King, who had not planned to go to the communal dinner, stepped out of a shower to enter the scene. "They got my brother," he sobbed repeatedly.

Shortly before the shooting, three squad cars full of police officers had stopped for a break at the fire station where Willie Richmond was surveilling King. An idle firefighter borrowing the officer's binoculars actually witnessed the shooting. Within seconds Richmond raised an alarm that sent 12 policemen running across Mulberry Street toward the motel. Their arrival added momentary panic to the people still processing events in the parking lot. Were the police storming the motel in an attack? Struggling to redirect the charging officers, people shouted that the shot had been fired from behind this advancing force. Richmond alerted police headquarters, too, and more officers descended on the scene.

In the brief time it took for reinforcements to arrive and surround the immediate neighborhood, Ray escaped. Panicked after glimpsing several policemen as he fled, Ray discarded the bundle that concealed his weapon and other possessions in a recessed doorway. Then he walked the remaining distance to his white Ford Mustang, climbed in, and drove off toward a nearby state line. Witnesses recounted these suspicious behaviors to police, but despite the broadcasting of an almost immediate alert about the fleeing suspect, Ray escaped detection in the ensuing confusion.

As Ray raced from the scene, an ambulance sped King to a local hospital where a team of doctors struggled to keep him alive. SCLC associates alerted Coretta Scott King in Atlanta that her husband had been gravely wounded. Before she could catch a flight to join him, she learned that, at 7:05 p.m., he had died. By then his assassin had long since crossed into Mississippi and was intent on fleeing the country. Just over an hour had elapsed since Ray had fired his fatal shot.

News of King's death flashed through Memphis, across the United States, and around the globe. It triggered widespread shock, disbelief, intense sorrow, unquenchable anger, and, on a smaller scale and in certain circles, delight. Movement leaders in Memphis hustled to prevent a violent backlash of local retaliation. James Lawson taped messages calling for restraint that played over local airwaves. He and others obtained police passes so they could cruise the streets and urge calm. Taking no chances, Mayor Henry Loeb imposed a new curfew and summoned a return of the National Guard forces that had decamped just days earlier.

After midnight Ralph Abernathy, other SCLC staffers, and James Lawson were among those who met in room 306 back at the Lorraine Motel. They fortified themselves for the path that lay ahead: staging the April 8 march as a tribute to their fallen friend, completing his plans for the Poor People's Campaign, and supporting the resolution of the Memphis labor strike.

Together, perhaps locking arms in the tradition of civil rights protests, they sang the movement's anthem, "We Shall Overcome."

Chapter 8

OVERCOME

"His face looked so young and smooth and unworried," observed Coretta Scott King when she viewed her husband's body on Friday, April 5. Clothing and skillful embalming masked his mortal wound.

King's widow and three of the couple's four children were among the thousands who converged on Memphis three days later to complete the fallen leader's wish for a peaceful march through the city. Charter flights arrived, filled with union workers. Political figures, entertainers, friends, colleagues, and civil rights veterans (including Rosa Parks) flew, drove, caught trains, or rode buses to reach the event. Locals turned out under the watchful eyes of thousands of National Guard soldiers. Whites who had never supported the strike—from ministers to housewives to members of the city council—mingled with union advocates, sanitation workers, and other African Americans of all ages and backgrounds.

Hold my hand while I run this race.
Hold my hand while I run this race.
Oh, Lord, hold my hand while I run this race,
'cause I don't want to run this race in vain.

*Verse from a spiritual sung in Memphis
during the memorial march of April 8*

Coretta Scott King (right,
marching in Memphis on April 8)
spoke about her husband's legacy
two days after his assassination
at the Lorraine Motel (left, police
on the scene following the
shooting). "The day that Negro
people and others in bondage
are truly free, on the day want
is abolished, on the day wars
are no more, on that day I know
my husband will rest in a long-
deserved peace," she said.

Students at all-black Hamilton High School reflected on King's death in classroom essays and poems. Many had attended the April 8 commemorations held at city hall (above). One girl wrote, "After marching in the Memorial March and listening to his courageous wife speak, seeing how she controlled her emotions, I got the courage to go on with life and struggle . . . to make something of myself."

"**March silently, in honor of the memory** of Dr. King," read the instructions that James Lawson had crafted for participants. "Sometimes silence speaks louder than words." Invaders, freshly trained in nonviolence, helped marshal a peaceful crowd estimated to be as large as 42,000. Hundreds carried memorial placards between their hands. The simple sound of thousands of shoes striking pavement accompanied the dignified procession. Arms linked in rows eight abreast, participants completed the march from Clayborn Temple to city hall that King had not been able to travel himself 11 days earlier. An outdoor program of singing, tributes, and speeches followed.

Coretta Scott King spoke last. "How many men must die before we can really have a free and true and peaceful society?" she asked. "If we can catch the spirit, and the true meaning of this experience, I believe that this nation can be transformed into a society of love, of justice, peace, and brotherhood where all men can really be brothers." The next day 150,000 people gathered in Atlanta for King's funeral, a three-hour assembly that was broadcast on national television, just as John F. Kennedy's funeral had been nearly five years earlier.

The morning after King died, as U.S. flags flew at half-staff in his honor, Lyndon B. Johnson ordered James Reynolds, a top official at the U.S. Department of Labor, to fly to Memphis immediately and force an end to the protracted strike. Even before King's burial, Reynolds began the delicate work of negotiating a settlement agreement. The eight-week-old walkout had long ago deteriorated into a stalemate. The two sides had barely talked since late February, and the few attempts to restart negotiations since had inevitably fizzled as labor reps butted heads with a mayor who still refused to recognize the workers' right to unionize.

Reynolds met separately with key players, then teamed up with local negotiator Frank Miles to inch the parties toward an agreement. Often they kept the sides isolated in nearby rooms and ferried suggested terms back and forth between them. As facilitators, they remained unbiased and thus built up trust among all parties.

Memphis avoided the wholesale rioting and destruction that
engulfed more than 100 cities around the country following the
assassination of Martin Luther King, Jr. It took federal troops to
restore order in Washington, D.C. (above and at right, scenes
of mayhem). Not since the War of 1812 had the nation's capital
faced such blazes; not since the Civil War were so many
federal forces required to restore order nationwide.

Throughout the negotiations, striking workers and their supporters kept meeting, protesting, and boycotting. Pinched business owners began to pressure the mayor and city council for a settlement.

By keeping the groups separated, they limited the fueling of the stereotypes and anger that had developed between the opposing forces, and they helped contain the hurt and blame that followed the death of King.

Throughout the negotiations, striking workers and their supporters kept meeting, protesting, and boycotting. Pinched business owners began to pressure the mayor and city council for a settlement. So did others who winced as *Time* magazine labeled Memphis a "decaying Mississippi River town," and groups began canceling plans to hold conventions in the city. Both sides worried that fresh violence could break out at any instant. By now pairs of heavily armed police officers guarded city hall, and Loeb kept a shotgun stowed under his desk.

MUCH OF the violent reaction to this bloody murder could be blunted if in every city and town there would now be a resolve to remove what remains of injustice and racial prejudice from schools, from training and job opportunities, from housing and community life.

Ralph McGill, editor of the *Atlanta Constitution*, in a column published April 5, 1968

On Friday, April 5, an interracial delegation of some 150 ministers marched to city hall and urged Henry Loeb to act. The mayor continued to justify his position by citing impressive tallies from his supportive mail, although more critical letters began appearing in the Memphis newspapers, and local news coverage became less inflammatory. The *Wall Street Journal* suggested the Memphis leadership was "out of touch but doesn't know it."

Reynolds held labor and city representatives captive at the bargaining table almost without pause for ten days. Finally, on Monday, April 15, exactly a week after the memorial march in Memphis, the details of an agreement began to emerge. "I think we would still be negotiating had it not been for him,"

Bill Lucy from AFSCME joked about Reynolds years later. Reynolds designed the settlement so that it needed approval by the workers and the city council only, thus allowing the mayor to save face as having held his ground. "The mayor didn't change his attitude," recalled Reynolds. "He didn't capitulate one bit."

The agreement's emerging language recognized the union, established a system for collecting union dues, promised job promotions without regard to race, and developed a plan for addressing future worker grievances. Workers had to promise not to strike again, and AFSCME waived its right to be the sole representative for the workers. The city agreed to a two-part pay raise totaling 15 cents an hour.

Representatives sought approval of the agreement on day 65 of the strike, Tuesday, April 16. At the city council meeting, one member objected because he felt the city could not afford the agreement's wage increases. At least one pointed out that strikingly similar deals had appeared within weeks of the start of the strike, but the council had failed to embrace them. This time members voted 12 to 1 to accept a settlement.

Earlier that day union reps had taken the unusual step of asking leaders from COME to endorse the agreement before it went to the workers for a vote. The ministers did, assuring unified support of the deal in the African-American community. Jerry Wurf and other AFSCME union officials caught up with striking workers that afternoon at Clayborn Temple as they prepared for a daily march. Wurf and Bill Lucy read the agreement aloud and explained each point to the assembled strikers. Then T. O. Jones, who had spent years fighting in Memphis for the rights of public employees to unionize, asked the men to vote. "All those who approve the agreement, please stand," he requested. No one remained seated to oppose it. "The motion has carried!" proclaimed Jones, his face streaked with tears of joy.

Workers and labor leaders, ministers and other supporters cheered and celebrated with handshakes, hugs, victory signs, dancing, tears, and laughter. James Lawson, who had been organizing the day's picket, described the transformed meeting as full of "great joy and happiness and bedlam." Before the crowd parted, those assembled joined hands and sang "We Shall Overcome," as they had at the end of every meeting throughout the strike. Wurf found himself crying along with others as they came to a verse they had sung throughout the struggle, even when only a handful of whites stood with hundreds of African Americans.

"Black and white together," they sang. "Black and white together today. Deep in my heart, I do believe, we shall overcome today."

n early May 1968, poor people from diverse corners of the United States climbed aboard buses, walked behind mule-drawn wagons, and converged by other means on the nation's capital. One notable contingent gathered on May 2 outside the Lorraine Motel in Memphis to begin its trek to Washington, D.C. By mid-May thousands had assembled at a homemade encampment on the grassy mall framed by the Washington and Lincoln Memorials. They called their settlement Resurrection City and hoped their presence and protests would prompt legislators to end poverty through job creation and social reforms. Inhabitants included Memphis labor advocate T. O. Jones, COME leader James Lawson, and Invader Charles Cabbage.

After the death of Martin Luther King, Jr., President Lyndon B. Johnson persuaded Congress to pass the Civil Rights Act of 1968, which addressed discriminatory housing practices, among other provisions. But Johnson's interest in waging the War on Poverty conflicted with the costs of the war in Vietnam. Organizational challenges, fatigue, ethnic and racial tensions, and bad weather all conspired to sabotage the Poor People's Campaign, too. About six weeks into the protest, local police borrowed a script from the 1932 bonus march and stormed the encampment after dark, attacking inhabitants with tear gas and clubs. Then they burned the city down. For all intents and purposes, the civil rights movement was over. By then a gunman had killed presidential candidate Robert F. Kennedy, brother of the slain John F. Kennedy. His death on June 6 added to the sense that the era of social reform was through.

And yet, by fits and starts, changes continued to ripple from the legacy of Martin Luther King, Jr. African Americans exercised their recently earned voting rights and began to elect people of color to represent them. In Memphis, for example, a youthful black teacher who had supported striking workers in

'' We can bring to birth a new world
From the ashes of the old
For the union makes us strong.
Solidarity forever, solidarity forever, solidarity forever.
For the union makes us strong. ''

*Excerpt from the labor movement anthem
written in 1915 by Ralph Chaplin*

I'M AVAILABLE FOR WORK

Every April 4, in keeping with the spirit of 1968 commemorations, activists rally to honor King, labor rights, and civil rights by retracing an adapted version of the historic protest route between Clayborn Temple and city hall (above, 1982).

1968 later won election as the city's first black superintendent of schools and, eventually, the first black mayor of Memphis. Blacks made gains in employment, education, business ownership, and quality of life, too.

The strength of labor unions multiplied after the Memphis strike as public workers around the country campaigned for union rights and won. Many repeated the Memphis cry of I <u>AM</u> A MAN in their protest signs. Ironically, one of Memphis's successful labor campaigns was made by the city's police force.

T. O. Jones once observed that the entire labor crisis of 1968 could have been avoided for the sum of about $44, the cost of the lost wages from the rainy

> **THE WHITE** community didn't realize that Martin Luther King was the best friend anybody had. He was the answer to the fire bombing and he was the answer to the looting and he was the answer to Black Power.
>
> **Lucius Burch**, white Memphis attorney who helped fight the injunction about the march of April 8, 1968

day of January 30. Instead, the city of Memphis expended nearly a half-million dollars paying for police overtime, related expenses, and the purchase of Mace, weapons, riot gear, and other supplies. Unions and strike supporters invested a comparable amount in their own operation. The state of Tennessee spent $1.5 million during the strike's two periods of martial law. Income lost during the boycott and property damages during rioting magnified the costs of the strike. Some of the strike's emergency trash collection measures (curbside pickup, weekly service, a five-day workweek) survived the walkout. The imposition of a local garbage collection tax helped cover the workers' increased wages; thus workers themselves funded some of their own pay raise.

Henry Loeb's term as mayor ended in 1972, and he never ran again for elected office. For years, resentments and racial tensions persisted between local blacks and police officers. A number of the Invaders ran afoul of the law, either for charges related to 1968 events or subsequent behavior. AFSCME officials moved on from Memphis to the next labor hot spots. In 1974 James Lawson relocated to Los Angeles, where he advocated for labor rights, peace, and social justice as pastor of a Methodist congregation. Ralph Abernathy led the SCLC until 1977. He and King lieutenants such as Jesse Jackson and Andrew Young maintained lifelong commitments to social justice. Coretta Scott King honored her husband's legacy through speeches, advocacy, and the development of the King Center in Atlanta, Georgia. She lived to the age of 78 and died in 2006.

Mason Temple, the site of King's two 1968 Memphis speeches, still stands as the headquarters for the Church of God in Christ. Clayborn Temple, the heart of the Memphis movement, endures but is shuttered and abandoned. A sports arena fills the space once bisected by the opening block of the 1968 route to city hall. When the historic Lorraine Motel faced destruction in the early 1980s, locals rallied to save it. Today the open-air balconies of the Lorraine serve as the façade for a modern structure that houses the National Civil Rights Museum. Exhibits surveying the full time line of African-American history reach an emotional climax with events from the labor strike of 1968, including a re-creation of the scene in room 306 during King's final motel stay.

A museum annex, located across Mulberry Street, has preserved the rooming house perch where James Earl Ray fired his fatal shot. Revelations of King-directed sabotage, Ray's conflicting accounts of events, and his cunning escape have fueled persistent suggestions that he did not act alone. Museum exhibits examine these conspiracy theories and outline the history of Ray's flight to Europe via Canada. The international manhunt required to apprehend Ray in London on June 8 matched the duration of the Memphis strike: 65 days. Ray never stood trial for King's murder because he pleaded guilty to the crime. A 1999 civil trial triggered by a suit from the King family supported the existence of a murder conspiracy. Ray never presented convincing evidence of accomplices, though, and he remained imprisoned until his death in 1998 at the age of 70.

In January 1986 the nation began commemorating Martin Luther King, Jr., with an annual federal holiday. The concluding "I have a dream" finale from his 1963 speech in Washington, D.C., has become inseparable from his image.

Many forget that these words arose from an event billed as a march for *jobs* and freedom, not just freedom. "Dr. King understood that political and social justice cannot exist without economic justice," Memphis strike supporter Bayard Rustin remarked after King's death.

President Lyndon B. Johnson had predicted in 1965 that progress for blacks could bring peace of mind to whites, too. He explained that segregation grew out of the false presumption by whites of their superiority over blacks. Evidence of that falsehood mounted during the noble, nonviolent advocacy of the civil rights movement. "Men cannot live with a lie and not be stained by it," observed the President. By admitting that lie and embracing the idea of equality, he said, whites "will find that a burden has been lifted from your shoulders, too."

But the realities of social change undercut Johnson's hope for a universal embrace of reform, and setbacks have unfolded alongside gains. Forces as diverse as competition in a global marketplace, increased mechanization, politics, and economic uncertainty have dramatically eroded union gains formerly achieved at great cost. Classrooms once integrated have resegregated as courts ended forced busing, white families migrated from urban areas to suburbs, and families of means supported private schools. Poverty continues to trap a disproportionate number of blacks in a loop of deprivation, crime, incarceration, and unemployment decades after the Poor People's Campaign.

"Freedom is not something that is voluntarily given by the oppressor," Martin Luther King, Jr., said in Memphis, yet he proved over and over again that it could be achieved through nonviolent means. His rich understanding of that truth arose from his relentless, uphill campaign for social justice. Two game-changing movements bookended that career: the Montgomery bus boycott that started in 1955 and the 1968 strike by the sanitation and street workers of Memphis. King's faith in nonviolence echoes through events that have unfolded around the globe in the decades since his death. Even at the dismantling of the Berlin Wall in Germany, people sang "We Shall Overcome."

Near the end of his life, King wrote, "The American people are infected with racism—that is the peril." He added, "Paradoxically they are also infected with democratic ideals—that is the hope." Those who followed King have seized that hope and worked to complete his dream for a humanity guided by its better angels.

Participants in the Poor People's Campaign (above, en route to Washington, D.C.) lived in A-frame–style plywood structures. Over time they added running water, electricity, food distribution, child care, health care, and garbage collection to their encampment.

The night before he died, King proclaimed that he had "been to the mountaintop." From the summit, he said, he'd "seen the promised land." His vision encompassed a world based on brotherhood, a land founded on equality, a people devoted to nonviolence. The civil rights movement may have sputtered and stalled after his death. Goals he set, including the eradication of poverty, may remain unmet. And yet, to use King's words, "we, as a people," have crept toward fairness, starting with the recognition of Local 1733 in Memphis 12 days after his death.

Born in 1929, King easily could have lived into present times. He could have watched southern communities close old wounds at the millennium by reexamining unsolved murders from the civil rights era. He could have witnessed the election in 2008 of the nation's first African-American President. He could have looked beyond our nation's shores and cheered the triumphant use of nonviolence during the Arab spring of 2011.

Were he alive today, Martin Luther King, Jr., would likely be pushing toward the next horizon, the newest measure of justice, the next reach toward that more perfect union that he observed as the promised land.

Were he alive today he would, no doubt, stand up straight and use his resonant voice to assure any doubters, all newcomers, every veteran of the fight to push on so that "We, as a people, will get to the promised land."

BEFORE THE STRIKE

TUESDAY, **January 30, 1968**
African-American workers in the sewer and drainage division of the Memphis department of public works are sent home with only show-up pay due to rainy weather.

THURSDAY, **February 1**
Memphis AFSCME organizer T. O. Jones introduces P. J. Ciampa, the union's national field director, to the new director of the department of public works in Memphis, Charles Blackburn.

Two Memphis sanitation workers—Echol Cole and Robert Walker—are crushed to death inside a garbage truck during a rainy afternoon of work.

FRIDAY, **February 2**
New York City sanitation workers go on strike. Negotiators reach a settlement nine days later on February 11.

STRIKE WEEK 1

SUNDAY, **February 11**
Hundreds of Memphis sanitation and street workers attend an evening meeting with union reps and decide to go on strike starting the next day.

MONDAY, **February 12**
More than 1,100 sanitation and street workers fail to show up for work, signaling the start of a labor strike.

P. J. Ciampa flies to Memphis that afternoon, upon hearing of the walkout.

TUESDAY, **February 13**
On Tuesday morning, AFSCME officials, including P. J. Ciampa, attend their first negotiating meeting with newly elected Memphis mayor Henry Loeb.

That afternoon striking workers attend their first organizational meeting; Ciampa speaks to the men for the first time.

Strikers march to city hall and take part in what becomes a confrontational meeting with Henry Loeb.

WEDNESDAY, **February 14**
Mayor Loeb breaks off negotiations with AFSCME officials and threatens to hire replacement workers if the strike continues.

THURSDAY, **February 15**
Memphis officials begin recruiting replacement workers to fill vacancies created by the strike.

FRIDAY, **February 16**
Union officials appeal to the city council for help in resolving the strike.

SATURDAY, **February 17**
Some 2,000 striking workers, family members, and other supporters gather at Clayborn Temple for the first community mass meeting in support of the job walkout.

STRIKE WEEK 2

SUNDAY, **February 18**
During Sunday services, striking workers appeal for support from the congregations of their local churches.

Late that evening, AFSCME president Jerry Wurf arrives in Memphis to personally assume responsibility for negotiations.

MONDAY, **February 19**
Jerry Wurf meets striking workers by attending their daily noon meeting at the United Rubber Workers union hall.

TUESDAY, **February 20**
AFSCME officials announce their backing of a proposed boycott of local white stores.

WEDNESDAY, **February 21**
Striking workers settle into the routine of three daily events: a noon union meeting, an afternoon picket march from Clayborn Temple to city hall and back, and an evening mass meeting with supporters at a local church.

THURSDAY, **February 22**
Members of the city council's housing, building, and public works committee, led by African-American chair Fred Davis, hold a public hearing in an attempt to craft a settlement agreement. Some 700 striking workers and supporters join the in-progress meeting and stage a sit-in—complete with a carry-in picnic—in an attempt to force an immediate settlement.

FRIDAY, **February 23**
Striking workers and supporters return to city hall in expectation of watching city councillors approve a settlement agreement, but no resolution is reached. The attempt by these disappointed masses to march to Mason Temple is disrupted as violence breaks out and police officers attack marchers with Mace and clubs.

SATURDAY, **February 24**
Some 150 African-American ministers meet at Mason Temple and organize a strike support group called Community on the Move for Equality (COME), with James Lawson designated as the group's leader.

STRIKE WEEK 3

SUNDAY, **February 25**
Expressing support for striking workers and their families—including through the collection of donations—becomes an added order of business during Sunday services at African-American churches.

MONDAY, **February 26**
COME leaders hold their first strategy meeting.

TUESDAY, **February 27**
Expanding on earlier efforts, some 300 picketers march from Clayborn Temple to city hall.

WEDNESDAY, **February 28**
Some 100 African-American women join 300 striking workers for the day's picket march through downtown.

FRIDAY, **March 1**
The Kerner Commission, formally called the National Advisory Commission on Civil Disorders, a group convened by President Lyndon B. Johnson and chaired by Illinois governor Otto Kerner, publishes a report on the nation's rise in urban violence.

STRIKE WEEK 4

MONDAY, **March 4**
Martin Luther King, Jr., announces a revised start date of April 22 for his anticipated Poor People's Campaign in Washington, D.C., to be organized by the Southern Christian Leadership Conference (SCLC).

Hundreds of white union members march with striking African-American workers during the daily picket through downtown.

TUESDAY, **March 5**
Nearly 500 strikers and supporters stage a sit-in at the week's city council meeting; eventually 121 are arrested and marched to the nearby jail.

STRIKE WEEK 5

MONDAY, **March 11**
Students respond to promotions by COME organizers and begin walking out of schools in a show of support for striking workers.

THURSDAY, **March 14**
Malcolm Blackburn, minister at Clayborn Temple, and five other protesters are arrested for physically blocking the movement of garbage trucks driven by strike-breaking replacement workers.

Almost 9,000 supporters and strikers gather at Mason Temple for the movement's largest mass meeting yet as national African-American leaders Bayard Rustin and Roy Wilkins visit Memphis to offer support of the walkout.

SATURDAY, **March 16**
Young people begin staging weekend pickets at downtown and suburban shopping centers.

STRIKE WEEK 6

MONDAY, **March 18**

Martin Luther King, Jr., addresses a packed Mason Temple crowd, adding his support to the strike effort.

FRIDAY, **March 22**

A freak dumping of 16 inches of snow forces the cancellation of a planned work stoppage and mass march that King was to have led.

STRIKE WEEK 7

SUNDAY, **March 24**

Local mediator Frank Miles initiates an attempt to break the strike stalemate by holding nonbinding negotiations between labor and city representatives. The talks fizzle within days.

THURSDAY, **March 28**

Thousands of strikers and supporters gather for an anticipated mass march to be led by King, but, after a delayed start, violence disrupts the march, prompting harsh reprisals by Memphis police.

In response to the violence, Henry Loeb imposes a nightly curfew on the city, and National Guard troops arrive to enforce a state of martial law in Memphis.

FRIDAY, **March 29**

Vowing to return later to lead a peaceful march through Memphis, King departs town and flies to his home in Atlanta.

SATURDAY, **March 30**

AFSCME organizer Jesse Epps meets in Atlanta with King and leaders of SCLC.

STRIKE WEEK 8

SUNDAY, **March 31**

King addresses an overflowing crowd at the National Cathedral in Washington, D.C., for what becomes his final Sunday sermon.

President Lyndon B. Johnson announces, "I will not seek, and I will not accept the nomination of my party for another term as your President," vowing to focus his attention instead to ending the Vietnam War.

MONDAY, **April 1**

Visitation begins for Larry Payne, shot during the events of March 28. His funeral follows on April 2.

TUESDAY, **April 2**

Mayor Loeb's curfew ends, and National Guard troops depart from Memphis.

WEDNESDAY, **April 3**

King returns to Memphis on a morning flight from Atlanta that had been delayed because of a bomb scare; he and his associates check in to the Lorraine Motel.

A local federal judge issues a restraining order that prohibits King and SCLC staffers from "organizing or leading a parade or march in the City of Memphis."

James Earl Ray arrives in Memphis after driving there by car from Atlanta and rents a room overnight at the New Rebel Motel.

Wednesday evening, despite a fierce wind and rain storm, King addresses a small but determined crowd at Mason Temple to deliver what becomes known as his Mountaintop Speech.

THURSDAY, **April 4**

That afternoon, James Earl Ray relocates his lodgings to a rooming house that overlooks the Lorraine Motel.

Just after 6 p.m., Ray shoots King as he stands on the balcony of the Lorraine Motel. King is pronounced dead at 7:05 p.m.

Mayor Loeb reintroduces his curfew, and National Guard troops return to Memphis for a new period of martial law. Riots break out at U.S. cities across the country.

FRIDAY, **April 5**

President Lyndon B. Johnson orders U.S. flags to be flown at half-mast until King's burial; he sends U.S. Labor Department undersecretary James Reynolds to mediate a strike settlement in Memphis.

Coretta Scott King flies to Memphis to retrieve her husband's body and bring it home to Atlanta.

SATURDAY, **April 6**

Strike settlement negotiations reopen with Reynolds serving as mediator.

STRIKE WEEK 9

SUNDAY, **April 7**

As many as 9,000 people attend an outdoor integrated reconciliation service on Palm Sunday afternoon.

MONDAY, **April 8**

Some 40,000 people gather in Memphis to honor King, promote racial understanding, and advocate for a settlement of the labor strike by marching peacefully from Clayborn Temple to a rally at city hall.

TUESDAY, **April 9**

King's funeral is held in Atlanta; 150,000 march through the city in his honor prior to the service. His burial follows.

For the second time Mayor Loeb lifts a curfew over Memphis and National Guard troops withdraw.

THURSDAY, **April 11**

The U.S. House of Representatives adds its support to the Senate-approved Civil Rights Act of 1968, the so-called Fair Housing Act.

STRIKE WEEK 10

TUESDAY, **April 16**

Negotiators reach a tentative settlement agreement on day 65 of the Memphis strike. The city council and striking workers approve the agreement that afternoon.

WEDNESDAY, **April 17**

Memphis workers return to their posts at the department of public works.

AFTER THE STRIKE

THURSDAY, **May 2**

A contingent of participants in the Poor People's Campaign gathers at the Lorraine Motel before heading to Washington, D.C., for the camp-in protest.

MONDAY, **May 13**

Participants begin occupying makeshift quarters on the National Mall in Washington, D.C., as part of the Poor People's Campaign.

THURSDAY, **June 6**

Senator Robert F. Kennedy, a presidential candidate, dies in Los Angeles, California, from gunshot wounds inflicted the previous day by an assassin named Sirhan Sirhan.

SATURDAY, **June 8**

Authorities arrest James Earl Ray at London's Heathrow Airport, ending a 65-day manhunt for the assassin of Martin Luther King, Jr.

MONDAY, **June 24, 1968**

Local police evict protesting residents from their temporary living quarters in Washington, D.C., and the Poor People's Campaign collapses.

THE DEAD

Echol Cole, crushed to death in a garbage truck on February 1, 1968, at age 36.

Robert Walker, killed with Echol Cole on February 1, 1968, at age 30.

Larry Payne, shot by police during the riots and looting of March 28, 1968, at age 16.

Martin Luther King, Jr., assassinated on April 4, 1968, at age 39.

Other deaths tied to the strike are those of Memphis black **Ellis Tate,** shot by police on April 4, 1968, during looting that followed King's murder, and **Lorene Bailey** of the Lorraine Motel, hospitalized the night of King's death because of a brain hemorrhage; she died the day King was buried, April 9, 1968.

KING'S CAMPAIGNS

Martin Luther King, Jr., campaigned tirelessly for civil rights during the final 13 years of his life. In some cases he helped to initiate the efforts (as with the Poor People's Campaign); in others, he responded to requests from local organizers to assist in their own grassroots operations (as with the Memphis movement). Eight notable campaigns are profiled here. Others worthy of recognition include Danville, Virginia, 1963; Chicago, Illinois, 1966; and St. Augustine, Florida, 1964.

Montgomery Bus Boycott

SETTING: December 5, 1955-December 21, 1956, in Montgomery, Alabama.

OBJECTIVE: To end the practice of segregated seating on the municipal buses of Montgomery.

ORIGIN: The strike begins after the arrest on December 1, 1955, of Rosa Parks, a local seamstress and advocate for African-American civil rights, when she refuses to move from the white section of a local bus to accommodate a white passenger.

PLAYERS: Rosa Parks, the Montgomery Improvement Association (MIA), Martin Luther King, Jr., Ralph D. Abernathy, other local ministers, African-American residents of Montgomery.

TARGETS: Local city leaders, owners of the Montgomery Bus Company, public citizens who advocate for segregation.

EVENTS ON THE GROUND: Martin Luther King, Jr., having recently moved to Montgomery to begin a career in the ministry, finds leadership thrust upon him as the president of the organization created in response to the arrest of Rosa Parks, the MIA. MIA supporters stage an African-American boycott of the local bus company that lasts for more than a year. Over time a complex and highly efficient system of carpooling helps to sustain the effort; after a local judge outlaws the shared rides in November 1956, determined supporters persist in their boycott by walking to their destinations for the final five weeks of the campaign.

OUTCOME: A Supreme Court ruling on November 13, 1956, declares the bus company's segregated practices unconstitutional. Five weeks later the ruling takes effect. Montgomery's buses become integrated on December 21, 1956. The Southern Christian Leadership Conference (SCLC), led by King, arises from the MIA and the successful boycott.

Albany Movement

SETTING: Fall 1961-Summer 1962 in Albany, Georgia.

OBJECTIVE: Local integration, especially of public transportation facilities, per the Interstate Commerce Commission ruling that followed the 1961 Freedom Rides.

ORIGIN: The Albany Movement blossoms following the arrest on December 10, 1961, of 11 people during an interracial challenge at the segregated train station.

PLAYERS: Youthful organizers from the Student Nonviolent Coordinating Committee (SNCC), local ministers and citizens organized under an Albany Movement banner, students at Albany State College, Martin Luther King, Jr., Ralph D. Abernathy, Bernard Lee, and other organizers from SCLC.

TARGETS: Local segregated train and bus stations and other examples of segregation.

EVENTS ON THE GROUND: SNCC organizers Charles Jones, Cordell Reagon, and Charles Sherrod use meetings and youth outreach to organize Albany support for tests of segregation. Their efforts build toward a series of mass arrests during December 1961. Local authorities struggle to find space in regional jails to hold all the protesters. As events build and movement organizers land in jail, locals pressure King to add his support to the movement. King delivers a pair of rousing addresses on Friday, December 15, and agrees to stay over and participate in a protest the next day. His arrest draws national media attention to Albany, but focus fizzles as tensions brew between SNCC organizers and SCLC newcomers. A hastily struck deal empties the jails but offers few local improvements. The movement continues in 1962 and features King's return (below) to face charges stemming from his original arrest.

OUTCOME: Despite setbacks, over time the Albany Movement advances integration goals, including successful voter registration drives. Albany serves as a reminder to King and SCLC organizers to be cautious about rushing into an ongoing civil rights campaign.

Birmingham Campaign

SETTING: April 3-May 10, 1963, in Birmingham, Alabama.

OBJECTIVE: Organizers hope to force an end to local segregation through the pressure of nonviolent protests.

ORIGIN: Wyatt Tee Walker, SCLC chief of staff, devises a blueprint for a focused, extended campaign in Birmingham at the request of Martin Luther King, Jr., and SCLC board member Fred Shuttlesworth, a minister in Birmingham.

PLAYERS: Shuttlesworth and other black Birmingham ministers; SCLC leaders including King, Ralph D. Abernathy, James Bevel, James Lawson, and Walker; and thousands of Birmingham citizens, especially young people.

TARGETS: Police chief Eugene "Bull" Connor and the white establishment of Birmingham.

EVENTS ON THE GROUND: The campaign builds more slowly than expected. King and Abernathy lead one contingent of protesters to jail over Easter weekend. During King's eight-day confinement he writes a defense of the campaign that becomes known as his "Letter from a Birmingham Jail." Soon after his release, an infusion of young people adds to the movement's momentum (above). Between May 3 and 7 thousands of them challenge local authorities during relentless phased marches and spontaneous pickets. The young people stand their ground even when attacked by police dogs and high-pressure fire hoses. Children as young as six join the movement and sing their way toward overcrowded jails. Images of the youths' courage and determination, even in the face of physical intimidation, attract a national spotlight on the city, forcing local officials to respond to protest demands. Details of an agreement are announced on May 10, ending the escalating protests.

OUTCOME: The agreement offers a timetable for rapid integration of public facilities throughout Birmingham. The successful campaign helps cement King's reputation as a national civil rights leader.

March on Washington

SETTING: August 28, 1963, in Washington, D.C.

OBJECTIVE: To mark the 100th anniversary of Abraham Lincoln's Emancipation Proclamation and to apply pressure for passage of civil rights legislation by the U.S. Congress, organizers plan a mass rally to be held in the nation's capital; they call it the March on Washington for Jobs and Freedom.

ORIGIN: Martin Luther King, Jr., proposes the idea for the march in early June 1963, and planning begins in early July.

PLAYERS: King and SCLC, John Lewis and SNCC, James Farmer and the Congress of Racial Equality (CORE), A. Philip Randolph of the Brotherhood of Sleeping Car Porters, Roy Wilkins of the NAACP, and Whitney Young from the National Urban League.

TARGETS: President John F. Kennedy, members of Congress, American public opinion.

EVENTS ON THE GROUND: A carefully executed plan mobilizes the transportation of tens of thousands of participants to Washington, D.C., on Wednesday, August 28. Hundreds of charter buses and 21 chartered trains help facilitate a diverse assembling of movement veterans, whites, students, labor representatives, and public celebrities. Participants gather at the Washington Monument and march to the Lincoln Memorial; by 2 p.m. a crowd of 300,000 or more has assembled for a three-hour program of prayer, music, and public speaking. King, appearing last, departs from his prepared text to share his dream for America, using threads of commentary from other recent appearances. Then he quotes lyrics from "My Country 'Tis of Thee" and adds rhetorical riffs on the song's theme to "let freedom ring." Following the peaceful rally, key African-American leaders meet for over an hour with President Kennedy to urge redoubled efforts toward the passage of a civil rights bill.

OUTCOME: Federal legislation finally earns approval in 1964 as a tribute to President Kennedy, who is assassinated three months after the March on Washington. King's Lincoln Memorial speech marks his place in history and adds to his prominence as a national figure.

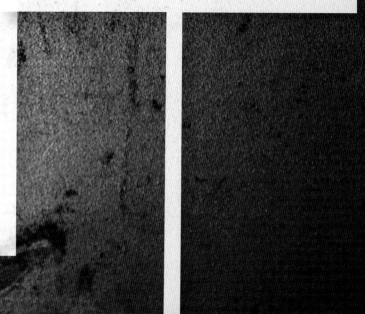

Selma to Montgomery Marches

SETTING: March 7, 1965, March 9, 1965, and March 21-25, 1965, over the 54-mile distance along route 80 between Selma, Alabama, and Montgomery, Alabama.

OBJECTIVE: To urge passage of a federal voting rights bill.

ORIGIN: The walk starts as a tribute to Jimmie Lee Jackson, a local black murdered on February 16, 1965, while supporting an ongoing Selma voter-registration movement.

PLAYERS: SNCC, SCLC, local advocates for voting rights, national volunteers, the federal government.

TARGETS: Segregationists, both elected officials and ordinary citizens, who stood in the way of enfranchising an estimated five million southern blacks.

EVENTS ON THE GROUND: The first attempt to complete the walk occurs on March 7. It becomes known as Bloody Sunday; some 600 marchers depart Selma and are attacked by a force of state troopers wielding clubs and tear gas as they cross the Edmund Pettus Bridge. Two days later, in the face of a court order preventing further walks, Martin Luther King, Jr., leads clergy who have gathered from throughout the county on a truncated march nicknamed Turnaround Tuesday because the group does not defy the march injunction. That evening local whites attack James J. Reeb of Boston and two other visiting white ministers. Reeb dies from his wounds. National news coverage and the endorsement by President Lyndon B. Johnson of the voting rights cause add to pressure for a completed march. The hike finally begins after its injunction is lifted. Federalized National Guard troops protect participants during the trek that unfolds beginning March 21. Waves of hikers take part, with hundreds or more participating daily (below). Three hundred complete the entire distance, and a crowd of 12,000 gathers on March 25 for closing speeches in the shadow of the Alabama state capitol in Montgomery. The day's successes contrast with the murder that night of Viola Liuzzo, a white volunteer from Michigan, during a high-speed chase along the route of the march.

OUTCOME: President Lyndon B. Johnson signs the Voting Rights Act of 1965 into law on August 6, 1965.

March Against Fear

SETTING: June 5-26, 1966, in the cities and countryside along a 200-plus-mile meandering route from Memphis, Tennessee, to Jackson, Mississippi.

OBJECTIVE: To march without fear through the heart of Mississippi at a time when whites routinely used threats of violence to intimidate people who advocated for equal rights.

ORIGIN: On Sunday, June 5, James Meredith, the first African American to enroll at the University of Mississippi, departs Memphis, Tennessee, intent on marching to Jackson, Mississippi, without fear of attack.

PLAYERS: James Meredith, Martin Luther King, Jr., SCLC staffers, Stokely Carmichael and representatives from SNCC, Floyd McKissick and representatives from CORE, supporters who travel to Mississippi in order to join the march, and local blacks who participate along the route.

TARGETS: Mississippi racists, authority figures in the South.

EVENTS ON THE GROUND: On day two of Meredith's march, a white segregationist ambushes the hiker with shotgun fire some 14 miles south of the Mississippi-Tennessee state line. Meredith survives but requires hospitalization. On June 7 civil rights leaders take up the march from the point where he was attacked. Their campaign continues despite public displays of white displeasure (above), inconsistent protection by state troopers, and attacks of marchers by whites and authorities (most notably the routing of some 2,000 marchers camping in Canton, Mississippi, by tear gas–firing police). On June 26 a recovering Meredith joins a crowd of 15,000 for the completion of the march.

OUTCOME: A gulf widens between King, who remains steadfast in his commitment to nonviolence, and younger leaders who advocate for more militant action. Stokely Carmichael introduces his cry for "Black Power" along the route. This rift and Carmichael's message draw media attention away from the more moderate King and undercut his influence as a national spokesperson.

Memphis Campaign

SETTING: February 11–April 16, 1968, in Memphis, Tennessee.

OBJECTIVE: Achieve union recognition for African-American workers in the city's department of public works, raise worker wages, improve workplace safety, create a grievance procedure, and eliminate discrimination in hiring, among other objectives.

ORIGIN: More than 1,100 members of the city's sanitation and street crews walk off their jobs on February 11, 1968, to advocate for union recognition and to protest the recent deaths of two sanitation workers, low wages, and a renewed policy that penalizes street workers on rainy days.

PLAYERS: Sanitation and street workers affiliated with AFSCME Local 1733, national AFSCME union leaders, local ministers organized through Community on the Move for Equality (COME), local youth (including members of the Invaders), labor mediators, Martin Luther King, Jr., and SCLC staffers.

TARGETS: City mayor Henry Loeb, members of the city council, Memphis police officers, local public opinion.

EVENTS ON THE GROUND: Key moments of violence and civil disobedience punctuate almost daily union meetings, mass meetings, and picket marches during the 65-day-long labor strike. Martin Luther King, Jr., visits Memphis three times to offer his support to what he views as a matter of economic injustice. Attempts to resolve the strike fail repeatedly, and the standoff becomes more and more racially charged. On two occasions peaceful mass marches turn violent: On February 23 police attack marchers with Mace and clubs, and on March 28 disgruntled African-American youths and criminals disrupt a march led by King, resulting in a violent pushback by police. Residents live through two states of martial law, the second of which follows the assassination of King on April 4 in Memphis. A federal labor official helps mediate an end to the strike stalemate on April 16.

OUTCOME: The negotiated settlement grants key worker demands, including the recognition of the right to be represented by a union. Unionization of public employees swells throughout the South and beyond.

Poor People's Campaign

SETTING: May 13–June 24, 1968, in Washington, D.C.

OBJECTIVE: Pressure members of Congress to pass legislation that would lift the nation's poorest inhabitants out of poverty through job creation and social welfare programs.

ORIGIN: Marian Wright, a young attorney and advocate for the poor, first suggests the idea to Martin Luther King, Jr., in September 1967. By January King has made the campaign the chief focus of his work through the SCLC.

PLAYERS: King, SCLC staffers, volunteers recruited nationwide to represent the diversity of the country's poor people, community leaders from the Native-American and Latino populations, and allies of the civil rights movement, both black and white.

TARGETS: Members of the U.S. Senate and House of Representatives, President Lyndon B. Johnson, news media, American public opinion.

EVENTS ON THE GROUND: Thousands of poor people and their advocates travel to the nation's capital and establish an encampment called Resurrection City on the National Mall. They stage protests (right), lobby legislators, and seek to create a functional  temporary city that respects the personal and economic well-being of its residents. Inhabitants reflect the diversity of America's poor, including African Americans, whites, Native Americans, and Latinos. King's assassination in Memphis on April 4 turns the campaign into a memorial effort. Coordination of the complex event proves problematic. Two weeks of rainy weather compound the logistical challenges, as do internal power struggles and mistrust among ethnic groups. In the end, local authorities close down the encampment through the use of tear gas and force.

OUTCOME: Federal lawmakers, short of funds because of a costly war in Vietnam, offer no legislation in response to the effort. The Poor People's Campaign represents the last major event in the civil rights movement.

While I wrote this book, tens of thousands of pro-union supporters swarmed the state capitol square in Madison, Wisconsin, some 55 miles from my home. They gathered to protest efforts by Scott Walker, the newly elected Republican governor, to strip the state's public employees of virtually all collective bargaining rights. Ironically, AFSCME (short for the American Federation of State, County and Municipal Employees), traces its origins to Wisconsin public workers who unionized in 1932. Some two decades later Wisconsin workers became some of the first in the nation to earn the same collective bargaining rights that public employees fought for in Memphis during 1968.

Thus, as I wrote this book, I time traveled between the union battles of 1968 and 2011. Watching the health of public worker unions hang in the balance in real time fueled my determination to recognize the gains—and terrible losses—that occurred in Memphis decades earlier.

My task of bringing that history alive would not have been possible without the foresight and hard work of Memphis residents who founded the Memphis Search for Meaning Committee within days of King's assassination. The vast archival record assembled by this team of volunteers undergirds every study made of the events of 1968 in Memphis. The initial work sprang from within the committee itself when member Joan Beifuss transformed her familiarity with the archive into the first book-length study of the history: *At the River I Stand* (St. Lukes Press: 1990). Years later labor historian Michael K. Honey undertook a new examination of the record, and his resulting volume *Going Down Jericho Road* (W. W. Norton & Company: 2007) stands as the definitive history of the topic. Both sources proved invaluable to my work. I am most grateful for Professor Honey's review of page proofs of my book, too.

During 2010 I spent the better part of two weeks combing through the materials collected by the Memphis Search for Meaning Committee. This vast archive, the Sanitation Strike Collection, is now housed as part of the Mississippi Valley Collection at the University of Memphis. Ed Frank, curator of special collections, could not have been more welcoming or helpful during my research, as were staff members Bridget, Jim, and Sharon. Their colleague, Chris Ratliff offered crucial help then and later on. During my visits, I combed through thousands of pages of oral-history transcripts, photocopied newspaper coverage from the era, reviewed pamphlets and newsletters, and read letters written during the strike. Then there were the photos. Hundreds, even thousands of them, most taken by professional photographers at the *Memphis Press-Scimitar*. This book could not exist without the work of these eyewitnesses to history.

My greatest joy as a researcher came when I requested container nine from the Sanitation Strike Collection. As I unpacked the oversize archival carton I flipped through original sign placards from 1968 picket marches: "Honor King: End Racism!" "Union Justice Now!" "lest we forget . . ." And there, nestled among them, rested a card bearing the words I <u>AM</u> A MAN. A talisman of history. An object that yanked me straight back to 1968 when someone wearing this sign may have marched on Beale Street, perhaps in the face of bayonet-armed troops from the National Guard.

I found additional riches at the Memphis and Shelby County Room of the Memphis Public Library thanks to the help of librarian Marilyn Umfress and archivist G. Wayne Dowdy. A special find there was an original FBI wanted poster for James Earl Ray (on page 75). Many Memphians made me feel at home during my research trips. Special thanks go to Andrew and Perry Withers (sons of noted civil rights photographer Ernest C. Withers); Andrew's wife, Cheri Withers; retired sanitation worker Taylor Rogers and his wife, Bessie Rogers; Katral K. Rainey of the Gospel Temple Baptist Church; Samuel and Juanita Chambers; Cathy Evans of St. Mary's Episcopal

School and her husband, John Evans; Kim Ford of Cypress Middle School, her students in 7-5, and other local educators and students.

During this project I enjoyed returning to authors and sources from my earlier look at civil rights history, *Freedom Riders* (National Geographic: 2006). This time I consulted all three volumes of Taylor Branch's indispensible biography of Martin Luther King, Jr., especially the final book of the series, *At Canaan's Edge* (Simon & Schuster: 2006). Other familiar sources included *Voices of Freedom* by Henry Hampton and Steve Fayer (Bantam Books: 1990); *I'm Gonna Let It Shine* by Bill Harley (Round River Records: 1990);

and *Everybody Says Freedom* by Pete Seeger and Bob Reiser (W. W. Norton & Company: 1989).

Additional notable sources included Philip Dray's history of U.S. labor unions, *There Is Power in a Union* (Doubleday: 2010); *Hellhound on His Trail,* the detailed study of James Earl Ray by Hampton Sides (Doubleday: 2010); Gene Roberts and Hank Klibanoff's thoughtful study of media coverage during the civil rights era, *The Race Beat* (Knopf: 2006); and *There Goes My Everything,* Jason Sokol's study of the evolving racial mind-set of southern whites (Knopf: 2006). For a full list of works consulted, see the accompanying bibliography.

Acknowledgments

Each year I grow more indebted to the family, friends, and colleagues who support my work and cut me slack when I disappear from view to immerse myself in the past. Thanks once again for welcoming me back to present times without rebuke. Hats off to Jake and Sam who keep growing up well, whether I'm watching or distracted. As always, I draw inspiration and pleasure from my parents Dolores and Henry, my brother David, his wife Mary, and so many friends near and far. My critique partners—Georgia Beaverson, Pam Beres, Judy Bryan, Elizabeth Fixmer, and Jamie Swenson—give far more than an equal measure of what I can offer in return: Thank you!

This book marks my ninth straight collaboration with Jennifer Emmett at National Geographic Children's Books, and once again she's made all the work seem like play. Kudos to designer Marty Ittner for her ceaseless creativity and ingenuity; you've outdone yourself this time, Marty! Thanks to the whole production team, too, including Lori Epstein, Eva Absher, Nancy Laties Feresten, Lewis R. Bassford, Grace Hill, Joan Gossett, Kathryn Robbins, Kate Olesin, and Susan Borke.

When King died in 1968, I was ten years old and a student in fifth grade. Just the previous year my Virginia school district had integrated its facilities. My family was one of a handful that did not opt out of having white children placed in a classroom led by an African-American teacher. How fortunate I was to have Mrs. Christine Warren as my teacher. Integration came with not inconsiderable growing pains—the initial segregation of classrooms led by African-American teachers, for example, both geographically and during social periods such as recess and lunchtime—but Mrs. Warren focused on academics, not distractions, and I had a positive year. Only eight or nine at the time, I remained oblivious to the races of fellow students and teachers. My memories are of book reports, and starting a stamp collection, and learning how to compose a letter. And that's just how it should be. Thank you, Mrs. Warren!

Books of General Interest

Bolden, Tonya. *M.L.K.: Journey of a King.* New York: Abrams Books for Young Readers, 2007.

Honey, Michael K. *All Labor Has Dignity.* Boston: Beacon Press, 2011.

———. *Going Down Jericho Road: The Memphis Strike, Martin Luther King's Last Campaign.* New York: W. W. Norton & Company, 2007.

I Am a Man: Photographs of the 1968 Memphis Sanitation Strike and Dr. Martin Luther King, Jr. Memphis: Memphis Publishing Company, 1993.

Kasher, Steven. *The Civil Rights Movement: A Photographic History, 1954-68.* New York: Abbeville Press, 2000.

King, Jr., Martin Luther. *I Have a Dream: Writings and Speeches That Changed the World.* Edited by James M. Washington. San Francisco: HarperSanFrancisco, 1992.

Sides, Hampton. *Hellhound on His Trail: The Stalking of Martin Luther King, Jr. and the International Hunt for His Assassin.* New York: Doubleday, 2010.

Music

If I Had a Hammer: Songs of Hope and Struggle
Performed by Pete Seeger
Smithsonian Folkways: 1998

I'm Gonna Let It Shine: A Gathering of Voices for Freedom
Round River Records: 1990

Documentary Films

At the River I Stand
Memphis State University: 1993

I AM A MAN
Memphis Tourism
Foundation: 2009
http://www.iamamanthemovie.com/

Background interviews: http://vimeo.com/14935109

Curriculum guide: http://www.iamamanthemovie.com/guide/

The Witness
National Civil Rights Museum: 2009

Places to Visit in Person and Online

"The African American Odyssey: A Quest for Full Citizenship"
Online exhibit through American Memory, Library of Congress
Full exhibit: http://memory.loc.gov/ammem/aaohtml/exhibit/aointro.html

Chapter IX: "The Civil Rights Era"
http://memory.loc.gov/ammem/aaohtml/exhibit/aopart9.html

"AFSCME and Dr. King"
American Federation of State, County and Municipal Employees (AFSCME) Online archive:
http://www.afscme.org/about/1029.cfm

"Dr. Martin Luther King Jr.—1968" *Commercial Appeal*
Online archive: http://www.commercialappeal.com/news/mlk/

"Fighting for Working Families: A Short History of AFSCME"
Online brochure:
http://www.afscme.org/docs/afscme_history.pdf

The King Center
Atlanta, Georgia
http://www.thekingcenter.org/Default.aspx

Memphis, Tennessee
http://www.memphistravel.com/

National Civil Rights Museum
Memphis, Tennessee
http://www.civilrightsmuseum.org/home.htm

National Park Service
We Shall Overcome: Historic Places of the Civil Rights Movement—A National Register of Historic Places Travel Itinerary
http://www.nps.gov/nr/travel/civilrights/

Mason Temple: http://www.nps.gov/nr/travel/civilrights/tn1.htm

Lorraine Motel: http://www.nps.gov/nr/travel/civilrights/tn2.htm

Smithsonian National Museum of African American History and Culture
Washington, D.C.
http://nmaahc.si.edu/

Ernest C. Withers Photography Collection
http://nmaahc.si.edu/section/collections/view/97

Southern Christian Leadership Conference (SCLC)
Homepage: http://sclcnational.org/

SCLC history: http://sclcnational.org/item/25461

Abernathy, Ralph D., letter to SCLC friends, June 1968. Sanitation Strike Collection of the Mississippi Valley Collection: Container 6, Folder 30.

Beifuss, Joan Turner. *At the River I Stand.* Memphis: St. Lukes Press, 1990.

Beik, Millie Allen. "The Memphis Sanitation Strike of 1968." In *Labor Relations,* 223-48. Westport, CT: Greenwood Press, 2005.

Branch, Taylor. *At Canaan's Edge: America in the King Years, 1965-68.* New York: Simon & Schuster, 2006.

————. *Parting the Waters: America in the King Years, 1954-63.* New York: Simon & Schuster, 1988.

————. *Pillar of Fire: America in the King Years, 1963-65.* New York: Simon & Schuster, 1998.

Caldwell, Earl. "Abernathy Takes Civil Rights Post Held by Dr. King and Pledges Nonviolence." *New York Times,* April 6, 1968.

————. "Abernathy, in Memphis, Pledges 'Militant Action.'" *New York Times,* April 16, 1968.

————. "After King: His Deputy Carries On His Work." *New York Times,* April 21, 1968.

————. "Guard Called Out." *New York Times,* April 5, 1968, 1, 24.

————. "Memphis Protest Avoids Violence." *New York Times,* March 24, 1968.

————. "Mrs. King to March in Husband's Place in Memphis Today." *New York Times,* April 8, 1968, 1, 33.

————. "Negroes to Seek More in Memphis." *New York Times,* April 21, 1968.

Cohen, Patricia. "'Culture of Poverty' Makes a Comeback." *New York Times,* October 17, 2010.

Committee on the Move for Equality (COME), Memphis, Tennessee. Flyer, "Be Cool, Fool!!"

March 1968. Sanitation Strike Collection of the Mississippi Valley Collection: Container 5, Folder 14.

Dray, Philip. *There Is Power in a Union: The Epic Story of Labor in America.* New York: Doubleday, 2010.

Estes, Steve. *I Am a Man!: Race, Manhood, and the Civil Rights Movement.* Chapel Hill: The University of North Carolina Press, 2005.

Green, Archie, David Roediger, Franklin Rosemont, Salvatore Salerno, eds. *The Big Red Songbook.* Chicago: Charles H. Kerr Publishing Company, 2007.

Hampton, Henry and Steve Fayer. *Voices of Freedom: An Oral History of the Civil Rights Movement from the 1950s through the 1980s.* New York: Bantam Books, 1990.

Harley, Bill. *I'm Gonna Let It Shine: A Gathering of Voices for Freedom.* Seekonk, MA: Round River Records, 1990.

The Holy Bible. Nashville: Thomas Nelson Publishers, 1990.

Honey, Michael K. *All Labor Has Dignity.* Boston: Beacon Press, 2011.

————. *Black Workers Remember: An Oral History of Segregation, Unionism, and the Freedom Struggle.* Berkeley: University of California Press, 1999.

————. *Going Down Jericho Road: The Memphis Strike, Martin Luther King's Last Campaign.* New York: W. W. Norton & Company, 2007.

Hurley, F. Jack. "Photographing Struggle, Building Bridges." In *Pictures Tell the Story: Ernest C. Withers Reflections in History.* Norfolk, VA: Chrysler Museum of Art, 2000.

I Am a Man: Photographs of the 1968 Memphis Sanitation Strike and Dr. Martin Luther King, Jr. Memphis: Memphis Publishing Company, 1993.

Johnson, Earnestine. Student essay written in Memphis, Tennessee. "Students' Responses to Assassination," Spring 1968. Sanitation Strike Collection of the Mississippi Valley Collection: Container 8, Folder 51.

King, Jr., Martin Luther. *I Have a Dream: Writings and Speeches That Changed the World.* Edited by James M. Washington. San Francisco: HarperSanFrancisco, 1992.

————. Letter to SCLC supporters, February 15, 1968. Sanitation Strike Collection of the Mississippi Valley Collection: Container 6, Folder 30.

Lawson, James. Memo of instructions to marchers, April 8, 1968. Sanitation Strike Collection of the Mississippi Valley Collection: Container 5, Folder 14.

Leisy, James F. *The Good Times Songbook.* Nashville: Abingdon Press, 1974.

Lentz, Richard. "Committee Gives in to Sit-In of Strikers, but Loeb Holds Firm." *Commercial Appeal* (Memphis), February 23, 1968, 1.

"The March on Main." *Commercial Appeal* (Memphis), February 24, 1968, 6.

Memphis Taxpayer, letter to Henry Loeb, March 24, 1968. Papers of Henry Loeb, Memphis and Shelby County Room, Memphis Public Library: Series III, Box 238, Folder 6, Sanitation Strike.

"Mississippi Seeks Dismissal of Lawsuit on Secret Files." *Memphis Press-Scimitar,* October 2, 1980.

Porteous, Clark. "'I Was in Eye of the Storm': Porteous." *Memphis Press-Scimitar,* March 29, 1968.

Randall, Mary Helen. "I Am (Still) a Man." *Memphis,* April 2010, 28-33.

Risen, Clay. *A Nation on Fire: America in the Wake of the King Assassination.* Hoboken: John Wiley & Sons, 2009.

BIBLIOGRAPHY

Roberts, Gene and Hank Klibanoff. *The Race Beat: The Press, the Civil Rights Struggle, and the Awakening of a Nation.* New York: Alfred A. Knopf, 2006.

Rugaber, Walter. "Dr. King Planning to Disrupt Capital in Drive for Jobs." *New York Times*, December 5, 1967, 1.

Scroggs, Larry. "New Union Command Post Hints 'We're Here to Stay.'" *Commercial Appeal* (Memphis), February 16, 1968, 23.

Seeger, Pete. *American Favorite Ballads.* New York: Oak Publications, 1961.

Seeger, Pete and Bob Reiser. *Everybody Says Freedom.* New York: W. W. Norton & Company, 1989.

Sides, Hampton. *Hellhound on His Trail: The Stalking of Martin Luther King, Jr. and the International Hunt for His Assassin.* New York: Doubleday, 2010.

Siegmeister, Elie. *Work and Sing: A Collection of the Songs that Built America.* New York: William R. Scott, Inc., 1944.

Silverman, Jerry. *Slave Songs.* New York: Chelsea House Publishers, 1994.

Smith, Maxine. Oral history interview collected June 13, 1968, by Bill Thomas and Joan Beifuss. Sanitation Strike Collection of the Mississippi Valley Collection, transcription of tapes 147 and 148.

Sokol, Jason. *There Goes My Everything: White Southerners in the Age of Civil Rights, 1945-1975.* New York: Alfred A. Knopf, 2006.

"The Songs of Joe Hill." New York: Folkways Records, 1954.

"'Stiff' Bargaining Lips Flip Quips." *Commercial Appeal* (Memphis), February 14, 1968, 19.

Strike supporter, anonymous note to scab worker. Memphis and Shelby County Room, Memphis Public Library: Frank Holloman Collection, Series III, Box 6, Civil Disorders.

Thompson, Joseph. "Garbage Truck Kills 2 Crewmen." *Commercial Appeal* (Memphis), February 2, 1968, 1.

"Witness Tells of Man's Death." *Memphis Press-Scimitar*, February 2, 1968, 10.

A Note on the Design: The 1960s was a period of turbulence in America—filled with protests and marches, strong voices and, ultimately, significant change. The design of this book evokes the era with its typography and color palette and with its recurring motif of placards and protest signs. The colorized endpapers are inspired by protest signs from the 1968 Memphis sanitation workers' strike. The photo essay spreads (for example, pages 36–37 and 74–75) are constructed to evoke photo essays from the period as published in *Life* magazine. The large orange quotation marks throughout emphasize the primary source material and make the book feel like a conversation with history. Introductory lyrics add a soundtrack from the nation's notable protest songs for labor and civil rights. The texture used for color emphasis is meant to suggest urban decay and the dirty metallic of a garbage can. All the photography from the period is black and white; here, some of it is tinted with blue, orange, or green color washes to add drama and life. The text for the book is set in Adobe Caslon and Headline HPLHS and, incredibly, Memphis, a particularly serendipitous font choice.

CITATIONS

Introduction

SONG LYRICS: "Nobody Knows the Trouble I've Seen." (Leisy: 256).

Chapter 1 **Death in Memphis**

SONG LYRICS: "We Shall Overcome." (Seeger and Reiser: 8-9).

RAISED QUOTE: p. 17, Taylor Rogers: "There wasn't too much opportunity....take what I could get." (Honey, 1999: 294).

TEXT: p. 12, Mrs. C. E. Hinson: "It was horrible." (Thompson: 1); p. 12, Mrs. C. E. Hinson: "His body went in first...hanging out." ("Witness Tells of Man's Death"); p. 12, Mrs. C. E. Hinson: "The big thing just swallowed him." (Thompson: 1); p. 16, Clinton Burrows: Workers "acted like they were working... doing what the master said." (Honey, 2007: 100); p. 16, Ed Gills: "That's when we commenced starving." (Honey, 2007: 100); p. 17, Local judge: "All city employees...whatsoever." (Beifuss: 33); p.19 P. J. Ciampa: "a guy who didn't know a sanitation truck from a wheelbarrow." (Honey, 2007: 100); p. 19, Maxine Smith: "Nobody listens....demands a crisis." (Honey, 2007: 53).

Chapter 2 **Strike!**

SONG LYRICS: "Which Side Are You On?" (Siegmeister: 90-91).

RAISED QUOTES: p. 25, P.J. Ciampa: "We've got to stay together....a month." (Beifuss: 48); p. 28, Anonymous: "This is just a warning....Please, please." (Strike supporter).

TEXT: p. 20, T.O. Jones and Charles Blackburn: "I'm ready to go to jail." "Why are you going to jail?" (Beifuss: 42); p. 22, Worker: "He gives us nothing, we'll give him nothing." (Beifuss: 43); p. 24, Bill Ross: "I said, buddy....you do it yourself." (Honey, 2007: 108); p. 24, P. J. Ciampa: Jones "had to run to stay out front." (Honey, 2007: 102); p. 24, P. J. Ciampa: "Oh, put your halo...get realistic"; "Because you are...make you God." ("'Stiff' Bargaining Lips Flip Quips."); and "Keep your big mouth shut!" (Beifuss: 46); p. 25, Bill Lucy: "The men are here....Here they are." (Beifuss: 49); p. 28, Striking worker: "Just give me...I'll buy my own." (Honey, 2007: 117); p. 28, Henry Loeb: "Bet on it!" (Honey, 2007: 119); p. 28, Taylor Blair: "would turn over in his grave....what his daddy had said." (Honey, 2007: 111); pp. 28, AFSCME official Joe Paisley: "They stood in unison....not going back." (Scroggs).

Chapter 3 **Impasse**

SONG LYRICS: "Dump the Bosses off your Back." (Green: 177-78).

RAISED QUOTES: p. 34, Ed Gillis: "If the ministers.... no violence." (Honey, 2007: 259); p. 39, Ku Klux Klan telegram: "Memphis is on the verge...for God and country." (Honey, 2007: 267).

PHOTO CAPTION: p. 31, T.O. Jones: "Tell the guys.... that's the best salvation." (Honey, 2007: 499).

TEXT: p. 30, James Lawson: "Let's keep marching.... Keep going." (Honey, 2007: 202); p. 33, Gladys Carpenter: "Oh! He runned over my foot!" (Honey, 2007: 202); p. 33, police order: "Mace. Mace." (Beifuss: 111); p. 34, "Yeah, we'll..." (Honey, 2007: 203); p. 34, Jacques Wilmore: "At that moment...a black face." (Honey, 2007: 205); p. 34, police: "Move. Move. Move." (Beifuss: 112); p. 34, Marchers: "don't rub your eyes." (Beifuss: 113); p. 35, police: "a large...crowd." (Honey, 2007: 216); p. 35, *Commercial Appeal:* "We think Memphians...self-control they showed." ("The March on Main"); p. 35, Maxine Smith: "The garbage strike hadn't really caught on." (Smith: tape 148, page 4); p. 35, Jesse Epps: "This is no longer....community fighting." (Honey, 2007: 213); p. 35, Boycott slogans: "Keep your money in your pocket" and "Buy no new clothes for Easter!" (Honey, 2007: 220); p. 38, Henry Loeb: "bushel baskets" of letters. (Honey, 2007: 137);

p. 38, Lewis Donelson: "Henry, I don't think....other 40 percent, too." (Honey, 2007: 195); p. 38, James Lawson: "We will sit...put us out." (Honey, 2007: 261); p. 39, Blanchard: "fourth nigger." (Branch, 2006: 700); p. 39, protesters: "We want jail, we want jail!" (Honey, 2007: 263); p. 39, Roy Wilkins: "It's hard for whites.... bad ones just get worse." (Honey, 2007: 284).

Chapter 4 **A War on Poverty**

SONG LYRICS: "I'm on My Way." (Seeger and Reiser: 56-57).

RAISED QUOTE: p. 47, Martin Luther King, Jr., (MLK): "I'm not only concerned....black and white together." (Honey, 2007: 187-88).

TEXT: p. 40, Bayard Rustin: "How can you get rid of poverty....gonna get rid of poverty?" (Honey, 2007: 282); p. 42, MLK: "I'm on fire about the thing." (Branch, 2006: 652); p. 42, MLK: "We intend to channelize....until America responds." (King letter to SCLC supporters); p. 45, J. Edgar Hoover: "No opportunity...ridiculed, or discredited." (Honey, 2007: 93); p. 45, Taylor Branch: King "preached like a salmon fighting upstream." (Branch, 2006: 673); p. 45, Andrew Young: "war on sleep" (Honey, 2007: 174); p. 46, Henry Loeb: "Well, you're sweet...what you're talking about." (Honey, 2007: 318); p. 46, Jerry Wurf: "The goddamned mayor...out of people's hands." (Honey, 2007: 314); p. 46, Jesse Epps: "No one else can get in the house." (Branch, 2006: 718); p. 46, James Lawson: King "just lit up like a lantern." (Honey, 2007: 296); pp. 46-47, MLK, excerpts from 3/18/1968 speech in Memphis. (Honey, 2007: 298-303).

Chapter 5 **Marching in Memphis**

SONG LYRICS: "There is Power in a Union." ("The Songs of Joe Hill").

RAISED QUOTE: p. 52, unidentified woman: "Those damn kids....going to blow up." (Honey, 2007: 353).

PHOTO CAPTIONS: p. 51, letter writer ("a tax payer"): "Memphis has been good....let them go hungry." (Memphis Taxpayer, letter); p. 55, Calvin Taylor: "We were representing....the white man afraid." (Honey, 2007: 234).

TEXT: p. 48, MLK: "There are no masses in this mass movement." (Honey, 2007: 189); p. 50, James Lawson: "We've got the perfect work stoppage, though!" (Honey, 2007: 323); p. 52, Calvin Taylor: "considered a noble deed...cat beat you up." (Honey, 2007: 87); p. 52, COME flyer: "The only force...courageous, yet militant." (Honey, 2007: 310); p. 53, School flyers: "If your school...prove it!" and "Together...Baby." (Community on the Move for Equality flyer); p. 56, MLK: "Jim, they'll say I ran away." and "I've got to get out of here." (Honey, 2007: 345-46); p. 56, Clark Porteous: "like a battlefield." (Porteous); p. 57, James Lawson: "We are now saying....can we have order." (Honey, 2007: 362); p. 57, MLK: "Maybe we just have to give up...take its course." (Branch, 2006: 734).

Chapter 6 **Last Days**

SONG LYRICS: "Ain't Gonna Let Nobody Turn Me 'Round." (Seeger and Reiser: 74-75).

RAISED QUOTES: p. 63, Carroll Richards: "It is in your power....condemn you as a fool." (Honey, 2007: 321); p. 66, MLK: "We've got to give...go down together." (King, 1992: 199-200).

PHOTO CAPTIONS: p. 59, Calvin Taylor: "Nobody could be....fighting something." (Branch, 2006: 738); p. 61, Maxine Smith: "The boy looked so innocent." (Smith interview: tape 148, transcript p. 4); p. 65, "Ain't we.... today?" (Honey, 2007: 389).

TEXT: p. 58, Ralph Abernathy: "I had never seen him.... didn't know what to do." (Honey, 2007: 367); p. 60, *Commercial Appeal:* "Chicken a la King" (Branch, 2006: 745); p. 60, Coby Smith" "We don't have to organize.... they organize for us." (Honey, 2007: 371); p. 60, MLK: "what must be done....There is no other way." (Honey,

2007: 370); p. 62, MLK, 2-15-1968 in Birmingham: "Dives went to hell...never really saw him." (Honey, 2007: 187); p. 62, MLK, 3-18-1968 in Memphis: "If America does not....*she too is going to hell.*" (Honey, 2007: 299); p. 62, MLK, 3-31-1968 at National Cathedral: "We are coming to Washington....hearts and souls in motion." (Branch, 2006: 746); p. 62, MLK: "Either the movement lives or dies in Memphis." (Honey, 2007: 381); pp. 66-67, MLK, excerpts from Memphis speech of 4-3-1968. (King, 1992: 202-03); p. 67, James Smith: "There was an overcoming mood.... that we were going to win." (Honey, 2007: 425).

Chapter 7 **Death in Memphis, Reprise**

SONG LYRICS: "Oh Freedom." (Harley: 6).

RAISED QUOTES: p. 72, Andrew Young: "I would like to remind you....and the Southern Christian Leadership Conference." (Branch, 2006: 762); p. 76, police officers: "Where'd the shot...come from?" (Sides: 173).

PHOTO CAPTION: p. 69, MLK: "Mayor Loeb...need of a doctor. (King, 1992: 196).

TEXT: p. 68, MLK: "I'd rather be dead than afraid.... afraid of death." (Honey, 2007: 429); p. 68, MLK: "This is what is going to happen to me." (Honey, 2007: 452); p. 70, MLK, excerpts from 2-4-1968 speech. (King, 1992: 191); p. 70, MLK: "If they couldn't... protect me? (Branch, 2006: 725); p. 70, Coretta Scott King: "Martin didn't say...time was running out." (Honey, 2007: 452); p. 70, MLK: "like the old Movement days." (Honey, 2007: 433); p. 73, MLK conversation with Ben Branch: "like you've never played it before....play it real pretty." (Beifuss: 383); p. 76, Lorene Bailey: "Somebody done hit that old white truck." (Branch, 2006: 767); p. 76, A. D. King: "They got my brother." (Honey, 2007: 434).

Chapter 8 **Overcome**

SONG LYRICS: "Guide My Feet." (Harley: 22).

RAISED QUOTE: p. 84, Ralph McGill column: "Much of the time...and community life." (Roberts: 403).

PHOTO CAPTIONS: p. 79, Coretta Scott King: "The day that Negro people...rest in a long-deserved peace." (Honey, 2007: 454); p. 80, Earnestine Johnson: "After marching...to make something of myself." (Johnson).

TEXT: p. 78, Coretta Scott King: "His face looked so young and smooth and unworried." (Honey, 2007: 453); p. 81, Instructions to marchers: "March silently... silence speaks louder than words." (Lawson); p. 81, Coretta Scott King: "How many men must die.... really be brothers." (Honey, 2007: 481); p. 84, *TIME:* "decaying Mississippi River town." (Honey, 2007: 487); p. 84, *Wall Street Journal:* "out of touch but doesn't know it." (Honey, 2007: 484); p. 84, Bill Lucy: "I think we...not been for him." (Honey, 2007: 489); p. 85, James Reynolds: "The mayor didn't change....one bit." (Honey, 2007: 489); p. 85, T.O. Jones: "All those who approve....The motion has carried!" (Honey, 2007: 492-93); p. 85, James Lawson: "great joy and happiness and bedlam." (Honey, 2007: 493); p. 85, Verse from "We Shall Overcome." (Seeger and Reiser: 9).

Afterword

SONG LYRICS: "Solidarity Forever." (Seeger, 1961: 91).

RAISED QUOTE: p. 88, Lucius Burch: "The white community....the answer to Black Power." (Honey, 2007: 412).

TEXT: p. 90, Bayard Rustin: "Dr. King understood.... without economic justice." (Honey, 2007: 465); p. 90, Lyndon B. Johnson: "Men cannot live with a lie.... shoulders, too." (Sokol: 317); p. 90, MLK: "Freedom is not...given by the oppressor." (Honey, 2007: 302-03); p. 90, MLK: "The American people....that is the hope." (Branch, 2006: 746); p. 91, MLK, excerpts from Memphis speech of 4-3-1968. (King, 1992: 203).

Ann Bausum writes about U.S. history for young people from her home in Wisconsin and speaks at schools across the country about her work as a children's book author. In 2010 her eighth title with National Geographic Children's Books was released to starred reviews: *Unraveling Freedom: The Battle for Democracy on the Home Front During World War I.*

Bausum's books earn frequent recognition from librarians, peers, and reviewers. *Denied, Detained, Deported* received the Carter G. Woodson Award (secondary level) from the National Council for the Social Studies in 2010. Her 2007 book *Muckrakers* earned the Golden Kite Award as best nonfiction book of the year from the Society of Children's Book Writers and Illustrators. *Freedom*

Riders (2006) gained Sibert Honor designation from the American Library Association, and *With Courage and Cloth* (2004) received the Jane Addams Children's Book Award as the year's best book on social justice issues for older readers. These and other titles appear on numerous lists of recommended and notable books.

Other books by Bausum include titles about the nation's chief executives and their spouses—*Our Country's Presidents* (2009, third edition) and *Our Country's First Ladies* (2007)—as well as a photobiography about the intrepid explorer Roy Chapman Andrews (*Dragon Bones and Dinosaur Eggs,* 2000). Find out more about Bausum, her writing, and her author-appearance programs at *www.AnnBausum.com.*

INDEX

Illustrations are indicated by **boldface.** If illustrations are included within a page span, the entire span is **boldface.** MLK stands for Martin Luther King, Jr.

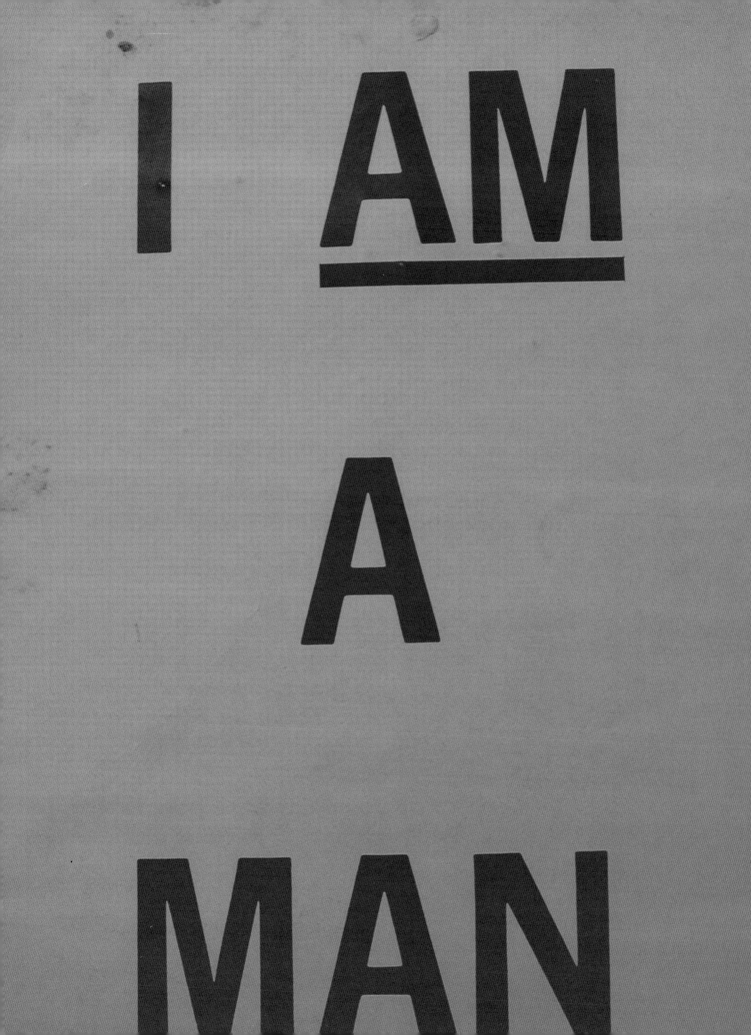

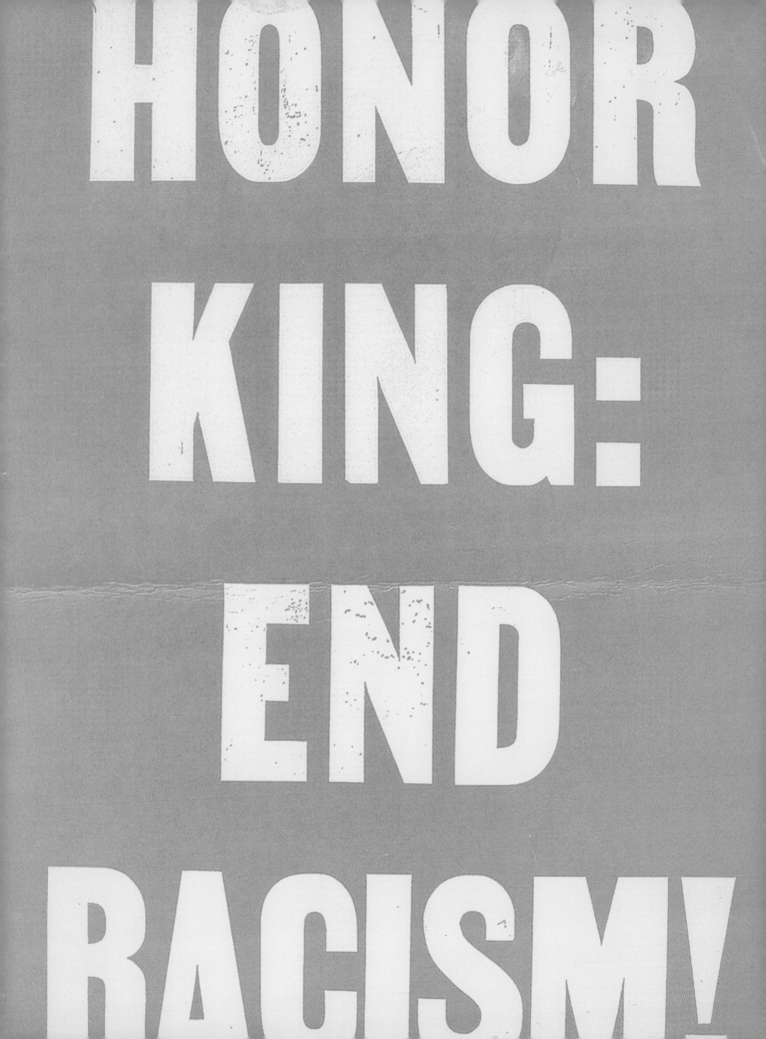